Furneaux Jordan

Body, Parentage and cCharacter in History

Notes on the Tudor Period

Furneaux Jordan

Body, Parentage and cCharacter in History
Notes on the Tudor Period

ISBN/EAN: 9783337043988

Printed in Europe, USA, Canada, Australia, Japan

Cover: Foto ©ninafisch / pixelio.de

More available books at **www.hansebooks.com**

BODY, PARENTAGE
AND
CHARACTER

IN HISTORY:

NOTES ON THE TUDOR PERIOD.

BY

FURNEAUX JORDAN, F.R.C.S.

LONDON:
KEGAN PAUL, TRENCH, TRÜBNER & CO. LIMITED,
1890.

PREFACE.

In my little work on "Character as Seen in Body and Parentage" I have put forward not a system, but a number of conclusions touching the relationship which I believe to exist between certain features of character on the one hand and certain peculiarities of bodily configuration, structure, and inheritance on the other. These conclusions, if they are true, should find confirmation in historic narrative, and their value, if they have any, should be seen in the light they throw on historic problems.

The incidents and characters and questions of the Tudor period are not only of unfailing interest, but they offer singularly rich and varied material to the student of body and character.

If the proposal to connect the human body with human nature is distasteful to certain finely-strung souls, let me suggest to them a careful study of the work and aims and views of Goethe, the scientific observer and impassioned poet, whom Madame de Staël described as the most accomplished character the world has produced; and who was, in Matthew Arnold's opinion, the greatest poet of this age and the greatest critic of any age. The reader of 'Wilhelm Meister' need not be reminded of the close attention which is everywhere given to the principle of inheritance—inheritance even of 'the minutest faculty.'

The student of men and women has, let me say in conclusion, one great advantage over other students—he need not journey to a museum, he has no doors to unlock, and no catalogue to consult; the museum is constantly around him and on his shelves; the catalogue is within himself.

TABLE OF CONTENTS.

NOTE I.—THE VARIOUS VIEWS OF HENRY VIII.'S CHARACTER.

	PAGE
Momentous changes in sixteenth century	1
Many characters given to noted persons	3
A great number given to Henry	3
The character given in our time	6
Attempt to give an impartial view	8
Need of additional light	14

NOTE II.—THE RELATION OF BODY AND PARENTAGE TO CHARACTER.

Bodily organisation and temperaments	15
Leading types in both	16
Elements of character run in groups	17
Intervening gradations	20

NOTE III.—HENRY'S FAMILY PROCLIVITIES.

Henry of unimpassioned temperament	21
Took after unimpassioned mother	22
Derived nothing from his father	23
Character of Henry VII.	24
Henry VIII., figure and appearance	26

NOTE IV.—THE WIVES' QUESTION.

Henry's marriages, various causes	27
Passion not a marked cause	28
Henry had no strong passions	30
Self-will and self-importance	31
Conduct of impassioned men	31

v.

NOTE V.—THE LESS CHARACTERISTIC FEATURES
OF HENRY'S CHARACTER.

	PAGE
Characteristics common to all temperaments	32
Henry's cruelty	33
Henry's piety	35

NOTE VI.—THE MORE CHARACTERISTIC FEATURES OF
HENRY'S CHARACTER.

Always doing or undoing something	37
Habitual fitfulness	38
Self-importance	40
Henry and Wolsey : Which led?	41
Love of admiration	43

NOTE VII.—HENRY AND HIS COMPEERS.

Henry's political helpers superior to theological	45
Cranmer	46
Sir Thomas More	47
Wolsey	49

NOTE VIII.—HENRY AND HIS PEOPLE AND PARLIAMENT.

No act of constructive genius	51
Parliament not abject, but in agreement	53
Proclamations	54
Liberty a matter of race	55

NOTE IX.—HENRY AND THE REFORMATION.

	PAGE
Teutonic race fearless, therefore truthful	56
Outgrew Romish fetters	57
French Revolution racial	58
The essential and the accidental in great movements	60
Wyclif	61
Erasmus, Luther, Calvin, Knox	62
Henry's part in the Reformation	64
No thought of permanent division	65
The dissolution of the monasteries	66

NOTE X.—QUEEN ELIZABETH AND QUEEN MARY.

Henry VIII. and Elizabeth much alike	69
Elizabeth less pious but more fitful	71
Elizabeth and marriage	72
Elizabeth's part in the Reformation	73
Elizabeth and Mary Stuart very unlike	74
Lofty characters with flaws	76
Mary's environment and fate	79
Bodily peculiarities of the two Queens	81

THE VARIOUS VIEWS OF HENRY VIII.'S

The progress of an individual, of a people, or even of a movement is never up, and their decadence is never down, an inclined plane. Neither do we see sudden and lofty flights in progress nor headlong falls in decadence. Both move rather by steps—steps up or steps down. The steps are not all alike; one is short another long; one sudden another gradual. They are all moreover the inevitable sequences of those which went before, and they as inevitably lead to those which follow. Our Fathers took a long step in the Tudor epoch, but older ones led up to it and newer ones started from it. The long step could not possibly be evaded by a Teutonic people. Rome lay in the path, and progress must needs step over the body of Rome—not a dead body then, though wounded from within, not a dead body yet, though now deeply and irreparably wounded from without. Civilization must everywhere step over the body of Rome or stand still, or turn backwards.

Two factors are especially needed for progress: brain (racial brain), which by organisation and inheritance tends to be large, free, capable; and secondly, circumstance, which continually calls forth capability, and freedom, and largeness. All the schools of supernaturalism, but above all the Romish school, compress and paralyse at least a portion of the brain : if a portion is disabled all is enfeebled. If a bodily limb even, a mere hand or foot, be fettered and palsied, the body itself either dies or droops into a smaller way of life. It is so with a mental limb—a mental hand or foot in relation to the mental life.

To the group of ever-present and subtle forces which make for progress, there were added in the sixteenth century seemingly new and conspicuous forces. The art of printing or writing by machinery sowed living seed broadcast over a fertile soil; the "new learning" restored to us the inspiring but long hidden thought of old Aryan friends and relatives, and this again in some degree relaxed the grip of alien and enslaving Semitic ideas which the exigencies of Roman circumstance had imposed on Europe with the edge of the sword. New action trod on the heels of new thought. New lands were traversed; new seas were sailed; new heavens were explored. The good steed civilisation—long burdened and blindfolded and curbed,—had lagged somewhat; but now the reins were loose, the spurs were sharp, the path was clear and the leap which followed was long.

While our fathers were taking, or were on the eve of taking, this long step, a notable young man, the son of a capable and wise father and of a not incapable but certainly unwise mother, stepped into the chief place in this country. A student who was in training for an Archbishop was suddenly called upon to be a King. What this King was, what he was not; what organisation and parentage and circumstance did for him; how he bore himself to his time—to its drift, its movements, its incidents, its men, and, alas, to its women—is now our object to inquire. The study of this theological monarch and of his several attitudes is deeply instructive and of unfailing interest.

The Autocrat of the breakfast table wittily comments on the number of John's characters. John had three. Notable men have more characters than "John." Henry VIII. had more characters than even the most notable of men. A man of national repute or of high position has the characters given to him by his friends, his enemies, and characters given also by parties, sects, and schools. Henry had all these and two more—strictly, two groups more—one given to him by his own time, another given to him by ours.

If we could call up from their long sleep half a dozen representative and capable men of Henry's reign to meet half a dozen of Victoria's, the jury would probably not agree. If the older six could obtain all the evidence which is before us, and the newer six could recall all which was familiar to Henry's subjects at home and his compeers abroad; if the two bodies could weigh matters together, discuss all things together—could together raise the dead and summon the living—nevertheless in the end two voices would speak—a sixteenth century voice and a nineteenth.

The older would say in effect: "We took our King to be not only a striking personality; not only an expert in all bodily exercises and mental accomplishments; we knew him to be much more—to be industrious, pious, sincere, courageous, and accessible. We believed him to be keen in vision, wise in judgment, prompt and sagacious in action. We looked round on our neighbours and their rulers, and we saw reason to esteem ourselves the most prosperous of peoples and our King the first, by a long way the first, of his fellow Kings. Your own records prove that long years after Henry's death, in all time of trouble the people longed for Henry's good sense and cried out for Henry's good laws. He was a sacrilegious miscreant

you say; if it were so the nation was a nation of
sacrilegious miscreants, for he merely obeyed the will
of the people and carried out a policy which had been
called for and discussed and contrived and, in part,
carried out long before our Henry's time. Upwards
of a century before, the assembled knights of the
shire had more than once proposed to take the property
of the Church (much of it gained by sinister methods)
and hand it over for military purposes. The spirit of
the religious houses had for some time jarred on the
awakening spirit of a thinking people. Their very
existence cast a slur on a high and growing ideal of
domestic life. Those ancient houses detested and
strove to keep down the knowledge which an aroused
people then, as never before, passionately desired to
gain."

"You say he was 'a monster of lust.' Lust is not
a new sin: our generation knew it as well as yours;
detected it as keenly as yours; hated it almost as
heartily. But consider: No king anywhere has been,
in his own time, so esteemed, so trusted, nay even so
loved and reverenced as our king. Should we have
loved, trusted, and reverenced a 'monster of lust'? If
you examine carefully the times before ours and the
times since, you will find that monsters of lust,
crowned or uncrowned, do not act as Henry acted.
The Court, it is true, was not pure, but it was the
least voluptuous Court then existing, and Henry was
the least voluptuous man in it. While still in his teens
the widow of an elder brother, a woman much older than
he, and who was also old for her years, was married to
him on grounds of state policy. Not Henry only, but
wise and learned men, Luther and Melancthon among
others, came to believe that the marriage was not
legal. Henry himself, indeed, came to believe that

God's curse was on it—in our time we fervently believed in God's curse. A boy with promise of life and health was the one eager prayer of the people. But boy after boy died and of four boys not one survived. If one of Catharine's boys had lived; nay more, if Ann Boleyn had been other than a scheming and faithless woman; or if, later, Jane Seymour had safely brought forth her son (and perhaps other sons), Henry would assuredly never have married six wives. You say he should have seen beforehand the disparity of years, the illegality, the incest—should have seen even the yet unfallen curse: in our time boys of eighteen did not see so clearly all these things." "Alas," the juror might have added, "marriage and death are the two supreme incidents in man's life: but marriage comes before experience and judgment—these are absent when they are most needed; experience and judgment attend on death when they are needless." "Bear in mind, moreover," resumes the older voice, "that in our time the marriage laws were obscure, perplexing, and unsettled. High ideals of marriage did not exist. The first nobleman in our Court was the Earl of Suffolk who twice committed bigamy and was divorced three times; his first wife was his aunt, and his last his daughter-in-law. Papal relaxations and papal permissions were cheap and common—they permitted every sort of sexual union and every sort of separation. Canon law and the curious sexual relationships of ecclesiastics, high and low, shed no light but rather darkness on the matter. The Pope, it is true, hesitated to grant Henry's divorce, but not, as the whole world knew, on moral or religious grounds: at heart he approved the divorce and rebuked Wolsey for not settling the matter offhand in England. All the papal envoys urged the unhappy Catharine to retire into a religious house; but Catharine insisted that God had called her to her position"—forgetting, we may interpose, that if He called her to it He also in effect deposed her from it. God called her daughter Mary, so Mary believed, to burn Protestants; God called Elizabeth, so Elizabeth exclaimed ('it was marvellous in her eyes'), to harass Romanists.

"But the one paramount circumstance which weighed with us, and we remember a thousand circumstances while you remember the 'six wives' only, was the question of succession. If succession was the one question which more than all others agitated your fathers in Anne's time, try to imagine what it was to us. You, after generations of order, peace and security—you utterly fail to understand our position. We had barely come out of a lawless cruel time—a time born of the ferocity and hate of conflicting dynasties. Fathers still lived to tell us how they ate blood, and drank blood, and breathed blood. They and we were weary of blood, and our two Henrys (priceless Henrys to us,) had just taken its taste out of our mouths. No queen, be it well noted, had ruled over us either in peaceful or in stormy times; we believed with our whole souls, rightly or wrongly, that no queen could possibly preserve us from destruction and ruin. It was our importunity mainly—make no mistake on this point,—which drove our king, whenever he was wifeless, to take another wife. His three years of widowhood after Jane Seymour's death was our gravest anxiety."

The newer voice replies: "You were a foolish and purblind generation. The simplicity of your Henry's subjects, and the servility of his parliament have become a bye-word. It is true your king, although less capable than you suppose, was not without certain gifts—their misuse only adds to his infamy. It is true also that he had been carefully educated,—his father was to be thanked for that. It would seem, moreover, that quite early in life he was not without some attractiveness in person and manners, but you forget that bodily grossness and mental irritability soon made him a repulsive object. An eminent Englishman of our century says he was a big, burly, noisy, small-eyed, large-faced, double-chinned and swinish-looking fellow, and that indeed so bad a character could never have been veiled under a prepossessing appearance. Your King was vain, ostentatious, and extravagant. With measured words we declare that his hypocrisy, cruelty, sacrilege, selfishness and lust, were all unbounded. He was above all an unrivalled master of mean excuses : did he wish to humble and oppress the clergy—they had violated the statute of premunire. Did his voluptuous eye fall on a dashing young maid of honour—he suddenly discovered that he was living in incest, and that his marriage was under God's curse. Did the Pope hesitate to grant him a divorce—he began to see that the proper head of the English Church was the English king. Was his exchequer empty—he was convinced that the inmates of the wealthy religious houses led the lives and deserved the fate of certain cities once destroyed by fire and brimstone. Did a defiant Pole carry his head out of Harry's reach—it was found that that Pole's mother, Lady Salisbury, was the centre of Yorkist intrigue, and that the mother's head could be lopped off in place of the son's."

The two voices it is clear have much to say for themselves. It is equally clear that the two groups of jurymen will not agree on their verdict.

It is commonly held and as a rule on good grounds, that the judgment of immediate friends and neighbours is less just than the opinion of foreigners and of posterity. This is so when foreigners and posterity are agreed, and are free from the tumult, and passion, and personal bias of time and place. It is not so in Henry's case. Curiously enough, foreign observers, scholars, envoys, travellers, agree with—nay, outrun Henry's subjects in their praise of Henry. Curiously too the tumult and passion touching Henry's matrimonial affairs— touching all his affairs indeed,—have grown rather than diminished with the progress of time. Epochs, like men, have not the gift of seeing themselves as others see them. Unnumbered Frenchmen ate and drank, and made merry, and bought and sold; married their children and buried their parents, not knowing that France was giving a shock to all mankind for all time to come. The assassins of St. Bartholomew believed that in future a united Christendom would bless them for performing a pious and uniting deed. We see all at once the bare and startling fact of six wives. Henry's subjects saw and became familiar with a slow succession of marriages, each of which had its special cloud of vital yet confusing circumstance. So too the Reformation has its different phases. In the sixteenth century it was looked on as a serious quarrel, no doubt, but no one dreamed it was anything more. Then each side thought the other side would shortly come to its senses and all would be well; no one dreamt of two permanently hostile camps and lasting combat. If personal hate and actual bloodshed have passed away, and at the present moment the combat shews signs of still diminishing bitterness, it is because a new and mysterious atmosphere is slowly creeping over both— slowly benumbing both the armies.

An attempt must be made here to sketch Henry's character with as much impartiality as is possible. But no impartial sketch will please either his older friends or his newer enemies. Although Henry came to the throne a mere boy, he was a precocious boy. In the precocious the several stages of life succeed each other more quickly than in others, and probably they themselves do not wear so well. When Henry was twenty-five he was little less wise and capable than he was at thirty-five or forty-five. At forty he was probably wiser than he was at fifty. The young king's presence was striking; he had a fresh rosy complexion, and an auburn though scanty beard. His very limbs, exclaims one foreign admirer, "glowed with warm pink" through his delicately woven tennis costume. He was handsome in feature; large and imposing in figure; open and frank in manners; strong, active, and skilled in all bodily exercises. He was an admirer of all the arts, and himself an expert in many of them. Henry had indeed all the qualities, whatever their worth may be, which make a favourite with the multitude. Those qualities, no matter what change time brought to them, preserved his popularity to the last.

Henry was neither a genius nor a hero; but they who deny that he was a singularly able man will probably misread his character; misread his ideals, his conduct, and his various attitudes. Henry's education was thorough and his learning extensive. His habit of mind tended perhaps rather to activity and versatility and obedience to old authority than to intensity or depth or independence. His father, who looked more favourably on churchmen and lawyers than on noblemen, destined his second son for the Church. At that time theology, scholastic theology—for Colet and Erasmus and More had not then done their work—was the acutest mental discipline known as well as the highest accomplishment. For when the "new learning" reached this country it found theology the leading study, and therefore it roused theology; in Italy on the other hand it found the arts the predominant study, and there it roused the arts. Henry would doubtless have made a successful bishop and escaped thereby much domestic turmoil; but, on the whole, he was probably better fitted to be a King; while his quiet, contemplative, and kindly father would at any rate have found life pleasanter in lawn sleeves than he found it on a throne.

It would be well if men and women were to write down in two columns with all possible honesty the good and the evil items in the characters (not forgetting their own) which interest them. The exercise itself would probably call forth serviceable qualities, and would frequently bring to light unexpected results. Probably in this process good characters would lose something and the bad would gain. From such an ordeal Henry VIII. would come out a sad figure, though not quite so sad as is popularly considered.

It is not proposed in this sketch of character to separate, if indeed separation is possible, the good qualities which are held to be more or less inborn from those which seem to be attainable by efforts of the will. Freedom of the will must of course be left in its native darkness. Neither can the attempt be made to estimate, even if such estimate were possible, how much the individual makes of his own character and how much is made for him. Some features of character, again, are neither good nor evil, or are good or evil only when they are excessive or deficient or unsuitable to time and place. Love of pageantry is one of these; love of pleasure another; so, too, are the leanings to conservation or to innovation.

In thought and feeling and action Henry was

undoubtedly conservative. His conservatism was modified by his self-will and self-confidence, but it assuredly ranked with the leading features of his character—with his piety his egotism and his love of popularity. To shine in well-worn paths was his chief enjoyment: not to shine in these paths, or to get out of them, or to get in advance of them, or to lag behind, was his greatest dread. The innovator may or may not be pious, but conservatism naturally leans to piety, and Henry's piety, if not deep or passionate, was at any rate copious and sincere. Henry, it has been said, was not a hero, not a genius, neither was he a saint. But if his ideals were not high, and if his conduct was not unstained, his religious beliefs were unquestioning and his religious observances numerous and stringent

The fiercer the light which beat upon his throne, the better pleased was Henry. He had many phases of character and many gifts, and he delighted in displaying his phases and in exercising his gifts. The use and place of ceremony and spectacle are still matters of debate; but modern feeling tends more and more to hand them over to children, May-day sweeps, and Lord-mayors. In Henry's reign the newer learning and newer thought had it is true done but little to undermine the love of gewgaws and glitter, but Henry's devotion to them, even for his time, was so childish that it must be written down in his darker column.

We may turn now to the less debatable items in Henry's character, and say which shall go into the black list and which into the white. We are all too prone perhaps to give but one column to the men we approve, and one only to the men we condemn. It is imperative in the estimation of character that there be "intellect enough," as a great writer expresses it, to judge and material enough on which to pronounce judgment. If we bring the "sufficient intellect," especially one that is fair by habit and effort, to the selection of large facts—for facts have many sizes and ranks, large and small, pompous and retiring—and strip from these the smaller confusing facts, strip off too, personal witcheries and deft subtleties—then we shall see that all men (and all movements) have two columns. The 'monster' Henry had two. In his good column we cannot refuse to put down unflagging industry—no Englishman worked harder—a genuine love of knowledge, a deep sense of the value of education, and devotion to all the arts both useful and elevating—the art of ship-building practically began with him. His courage, his sincerity, his sense of duty, his frequent generosity, his placability (with certain striking exceptions) were all beyond question. His desire for the welfare of his people, although tempered by an unduly eager desire for their good opinion, was surely an item on the good side. The good column is but fairly good; the black list is, alas, very black. Henry was fitful, capricious, petulant, censorious. His fitfulness and petulance go far to explain his acts of occasional implacability. Failing health and premature age explain in some degree the extreme irritability and absence of control which characterised his later years. In his best years his love of pleasure, or rather his love of change and excitement, his ostentation, and his extravagance exceeded all reasonable limits. Ostentation and love of show are rarely found apart from vanity, and Henry's vanity was colossal. Vain men are not proud, and Henry had certainly not the pride which checks the growth of many follies. A proud man is too proud to be vain or undignified or mean or deceitful, and Henry was all these. Pride and dignity usually run together; while, on the other hand, vanity and self-importance keep each other company as a rule. Henry lacked dignity when he competed with his courtiers for the smiles of Ann Boleyn in her early Court days; he lacked it when he searched Campeggio's unsavoury carpet-bag. He seemed pleased rather than otherwise that his petty gossip should be talked of under every roof in Europe. It is true that in this direction Catharine descended to a still lower level of bed-room scandal; but her nature, never a high one, was deteriorated by a grievous unhappiness and by that incessant brooding which sooner or later tumbles the loftiest nature into the dust.

Henry's two striking failings—his two insanities—were a huge self-importance and an unquenchable thirst for notoriety and applause. I have said 'insanities' designedly, for they were not passions—they were diseases. The popular "modern voice" would probably not regard these as at all grave defects when compared with others so much worse. This voice indeed, we well know, declares him to have been the embodiment of the worst human qualities—of gross selfishness, of gross cruelty, and of gross lust. These charges are not groundless, but if we could believe them with all the fulness and the vehemence with which they are made, we must then marvel that his subjects trusted him, revered him, called (they and their children) for his good sense and his good laws; we can but marvel indeed that with one voice of execration they did not fell him lifeless to the ground. He was unguarded and within reach. If the charges against Henry come near to the truth, Nero was the better character of the two. Nero knew not what he did; he was beyond question a lunatic and one of a family of lunatics. Henry's enormities were the enormities of a fairly sane and responsible man.

In order to read Henry's character more correctly, if that be possible, than it is read by the "two voices," more light is needed. Let us see what an examination of Henry's bodily organisation, and especially of his parentage, will do for us. In this light—if it be light, and attainable light—it will be well to examine afresh (at the risk of some repetition) the grave charges which are so constantly and so confidently laid at his door and see what of vindication or modification or damning confirmation may follow. Before looking specially at Henry's organisation and inheritance, I purpose devoting a short chapter to a general view of the principles which can give such an examination any value. It will be for the most part a brief statement of views which I have already put forward in my little work on character as seen in body and parentage.

THE RELATION OF BODY AND PARENTAGE TO CHARACTER.

NOTE II.

It is unwise to turn aside from the investigation of any body of truths because it can only be partial in its methods or incomplete in its results. We do this however in the study of the science of character. It is true that past efforts have given but little result—little result because they ignored and avowedly ignored the connection which is coming to be more and more clearly seen to exist between character on the one hand and bodily organisation and proclivity, and especially the organisation and proclivity of the nervous system, on the other hand. Those who ignore the bearings of organisation and inheritance on character are, for the most part, those who prefer that "truth should be on their side rather than that they should be on the side of truth."

It is contended here that much serviceable knowledge may be obtained by the careful investigation, in given individuals, of *bodily* characteristics, and the union of these with *mental* and *moral* characteristics. The relationship of these combined features of body and mind to parentage, near and remote, and on both sides, should be traced as far back as possible. The greater the number of individuals brought under examination, the more exact and extensive will be the resulting knowledge.

Very partial methods of classifying character are of daily utility. We say, for example, speaking of the muscular system only, that men are strong or weak.

But this simple truth or classification has various notable bearings. Both the strong and the weak may be dextrous, or both may be clumsy; both may be slow, or both may be quick; but they will be dextrous or clumsy, slow or quick, in different ways and degrees. So, going higher than mere bodily organisation, we may say that some men are bold and resolute while others are timid and irresolute; some again are parsimonious and others prodigal. Now these may possibly be all intelligent or all stupid, all good or all bad; but, nevertheless, boldness and timidity, parsimony and generosity, modify other phases of character in various ways. The irresolute man, for example, cannot be very wise, or the penurious man truly good. It must always be remembered in every sort of classification of bodily or of mental characteristics, that the lines of division are not sharply defined. All classes merge into each other by imperceptible degrees.

One of the most, perhaps the most, fundamental and important classification of men and women is that which puts them into two divisions or two temperaments, the active, or tending to be active, on the one hand, and the reflective, or tending to be reflective, on the other. To many students of character this is not a new suggestion, but much more is contended for here. It is contended that the more active temperament is alert, practical, quick, conspicuous, and—a very notable circumstance—less impassioned; the more reflective temperament is less active, less practical, or perhaps even dreamy, secluded, and—also a very notable circumstance—more impassioned. It is not so much that men of action always desire to be seen, or that men of thought desire to be hidden; action naturally brings men to the front; contemplation as naturally hides them; when active men differ, the difference carries itself to the housetops; when thinking men differ, they fight in the closet and by quieter methods. Busy men, moreover, are given to detail, and detail fills the eye and ear; men of reflection deal more with principles, and these lie beyond the range of ordinary vision.

The proposition which I here put forward, based on many years of observation and study, is fundamental, and affects, more or less, a wide range of character in every individual. The proposition is that in the active temperament the intellectual faculties are disproportionately strong—the passions are feebler and lag behind; in the reflective temperament the passions are the stronger in proportion to the mental powers. Character is dominated more by the intellect in one case, more by the emotions in the other. In all sane and healthful characters (and only these are considered here) the intellectual and emotional elements are both distinctly present. The most active men think; the most reflective men act. But in many men and women the intellect takes an unduly large share in the fashioning of life; these are called here the "less impassioned," the "unimpassioned," or for the sake of brevity, "the passionless." In many others the feelings or emotions play a stronger part; these are the "more impassioned" or the "passionate."

Character is not made up of miscellaneous fragments, of thought and feeling, of volition and action. Its elements are more or less homogeneous and run in uniform groups. The less impassioned, or passionless, for example, are apt to be changeable and uncertain; they are active, ready, alert; they are quick to comprehend, to decide, to act; they are usually self-confident and sometimes singularly self-important. They often seek for applause but they are sparing in their approval and in their praise of others. When the mental endowment is high, and the training and environment favourable, the unimpassioned temperament furnishes some of our finest characters. In this class are found great statesmen and great leaders. A man's *public* position is probably determined more by intellectual power than by depth of feeling. Now and then, especially when the mental gifts are slight, the less pleasing elements predominate: love of change may become mere fitfulness; activity may become bustle; sparing approval may turn to habitual detraction and actual censoriousness. Love of approbation may degenerate into a mania for notoriety at any cost; self-importance may bring about a reckless disregard of the well-being of others. Fortunately the outward seeming of the passionless temperament is often worse than the reality, and querulous speech is often combined with generous action. Frequently, too, where there is ineradicable caprice there is no neglect of duty.

The elements of character which, in various ways and degrees, cluster together in the more impassioned or passionate temperament are very different in their nature. In this temperament we find repose or even gentleness, quiet reflection, tenacity of purpose. The feelings —love, or hate, or joy, or grief, or anger, or jealousy—are more or less deep and enduring. In this class also there are fine characters, especially (as in the unimpassioned) when the mental gifts are high and the training refined. In this class too are found perhaps the worst characters which degrade the human race. In all save the rarest characters, the customary tranquillity may be broken by sullen cloud or actual storm. In the less capable and less elevated, devotion may become fanaticism, and tenacity may become blind prejudice, or sheer obstinacy. In this temperament too, in its lower grades, we meet too often—not all together perhaps, certainly not all in equal degree—with indolence, sensuality, inconstancy; or morbid brooding, implacability, and even cruelty.

I contend then that certain features of character, it may be in very varying degrees of intensity, belong to the more active and passionless temperament, and certain other features attend on the more reflective and impassioned temperament. If it can be shown that there are two marked groups of elements in character—the more impassioned group and the less impassioned group—and that each group may be inferred to exist if but one or two of its characteristic elements are clearly seen, why even then much would be gained in the interpretation of history and of daily life. But I contend for much more than this; the two temperaments have each their characteristic bodily signs; the more marked the temperament, the more striking and the more easily read are the bodily signs. In the intermediate temperament—a frequent and perhaps the happiest temperament—the bodily signs are also intermediate. The bodily characteristics run in groups also, as well as the mental. The nervous system of each temperament is enclosed in its own special organisation and framework. In my work on "character as seen in body and parentage," I treat this topic with some fulness, and what is stated there need not be repeated now. It may be noted, however, that in the two temperaments there are peculiarities of the skin—clearness or pigmentation; of the hair—feebleness or sparseness, or closeness and vigour of growth; of the configuration of the skeleton and consequent pose of the figure.

If the conclusions here put forward are true, they

give a key which opens up much character to us. They touch, as I have already said, a great range of character in every individual, but they make no pretension to be a system. They have only an indirect bearing on many phases of character; for in both the active and reflective temperaments there may be found, for example, either wisdom or folly, courage or cowardice, refinement or coarseness.

It must always be remembered, too, that besides the more marked types of character, whether bodily or mental, there are numberless intervening gradations. When the temperaments, moreover, are distinctly marked, the ordinary concurrent elements may exist in very unequal degrees and be combined in very various ways. One or two qualities may perhaps absorb the sum-total of nerve force. In the passionless man or woman extreme activity may repress the tendency to disapprove; immense self-importance may impede action. In the impassioned individual, inordinate love or hate may enfeeble thought; deep and persistent thought may dwarf the affections.

As I have said elsewhere: 'For the ordinary purposes of life, especially of domestic and social life, the intervening types of character (combining thought and action more equally, though probably each in somewhat less degree) produce perhaps the most useful and the happiest results. But the progress of the world at large is mainly due to the combined efforts of the more extreme types—the supremely reflective and impassioned and the supremely active and unimpassioned. Both are needed. If we had men of action only, we should march straight into chaos; if we had men of thought only, we should drift into night and sleep!'

HENRY'S FAMILY PROCLIVITIES.

NOTE III.

IF there is any truth in the views put forward in the foregoing chapter, and if history has at all faithfully portrayed a character concerning which it has had, at any rate, much to say, it is clear that Henry must be placed in the less impassioned class of human beings. When I first called attention to the three sorts of character—and the three groups of characteristics—the active, practical, and more or less passionless on the one hand; the less active, reflective, and impassioned on the other; and, thirdly, the intermediate class, neither Henry nor his period was in my mind. But when, at a later time (and for purposes other than the special study of character), I came to review the Reformation with its ideas, its men, its incidents, I saw at once, to my surprise, that Henry's life was a busy, active, conspicuous, passionless life. He might have sat for the portrait I had previously drawn. Markedly unimpassioned men tend to be fitful, petulant, censorious, self-important, self-willed, and eager for popularity—so tended Henry. The unimpassioned are frequently sincere, conscientious, pious, and conservative—Henry was all these. They often have, especially when capable and favourably encompassed, a high sense of duty and a strong desire to promote the well-being of those around them—these qualities were conspicuous in Henry's character.

How much of inherited organisation, how much of

circumstance, how much of self-effort go to the making of character is a problem the solution of which is yet seemingly far off. Mirabeau, with fine perception, declared that a boy's education should begin, twenty years before he is born, with his mother. Unquestionably before a man is born the plan of his character is drawn, its foundations are laid, and its building is foreshadowed. Can he, later, close a door here or open a window there? Can he enlarge this chamber or contract that? He believes he can, and is the happier in the belief; but in actual life we do not find that it is given to one man to say, I will be active, I will be on the spot, I will direct here and rebuke there; nor to another man to say, I will give myself up to thought, to dreams, to seclusion. Henry never said, with unconscious impulse or with conscious words, "I will be this, or I will not be that."

Henry VIII. took altogether after his mother's side, and she, again, took after her father. Henry was, in fact, his grandfather Edward IV. over again. He had, however, a larger capacity than his mother's father, and he lived in a better epoch. Edward, it was said in his time, was the handsomest and most accomplished man in Europe. Henry was spoken of in similar words by his compeers both at home and abroad. Both were large in frame, striking in contour, rose-pink in complexion—then, as now, the popular ideal of manly perfection—and both became exceedingly corpulent in their later years. Both were active, courteous, affable, accessible; both busy, conspicuous, vain, fond of pleasure, and given to display. Both were unquestionably brave; but they were also (both of them) fickle, capricious, suspicious, and more or less cruel. Both put self in the foremost place; but Edward's selfishness drifted rather to self-indulgence, while

Henry's took the form of self-importance. Extreme self-importance is usually based on high capacity, and Edward's capacity did not lift him out of the region of pomposity and frequent indiscretion.

Edward IV. was nevertheless an able man although less able than Henry. Like Henry he belonged to the unimpassioned class; he was without either deeply good or deeply evil passion, but probably he had somewhat stronger emotions than his grandson. In other words Henry had more of intellect and less of passion than his grandfather. Edward's early and secret marriage was no proof of passion. Early marriages are not the monopoly of any temperament; sometimes they are the product of the mere caprice, or the self-will and the feeble restraint of the passionless, and sometimes the product of the raw and immature judgment of the passionate. Edward deserves our pity, for he had everything against him; he had no models, no ideals, no education, no training. The occupation of princes at that time brought good neither to themselves nor anyone else. They went up and down the country to slay and be slain; to take down from high places the severed heads of one worthless dynasty and put up the heads of another dynasty equally worthless.

The eighth Henry derived nothing from his father—the seventh,—nothing of good, nothing of evil. One of the most curious errors of a purely literary judgment on men and families is seen in the use of the epithet "Tudor." We hear for example of the "Tudor" blood shewing itself in one, of the "Tudor" spirit flashing out in another. Whether Henry VII. was a Tudor or not we may not now stop to inquire. Henry VIII. we have seen took wholly after his Yorkist mother. Of Henry's children, Mary was a repetition of her dark dwarfish Spanish mother; the poor lad Edward, whether a Seymour or a Yorkist, was certainly not a Tudor. The big comely pink Elizabeth was her father in petticoats—her father in body, her father in mind. Henry VIII. in fact while Tudor in name was Lancastrian in dynasty, and Yorkist in blood. No two kings, no two men indeed could well have been more unlike, bodily, mentally, and morally, than the two Henrys—father and son. The eighth was communicative, confiding, open, frank; the seventh was silent, reserved, mysterious. The son was active, busy, practical, conspicuous; the father, although not indolent, and not unpractical, was nevertheless quiet, dreamy, reflective, self-restrained, and unobtrusive. One was prodigal, martial, popular; the other was prudent, peaceful, steadfast, and unpopular. He is said indeed to have been parsimonious, but the least sympathetic of his historians confess that he was generous in his rewards for service, that his charities were numerous, and that his state ceremonies were marked by fitting splendour. Henry VIII. changed (or destroyed) his ministers, his bishops, his wives, and his measures also, many times. Henry VII. kept his wife—perverse and mischievous as she was,—till she died; kept his ministers and bishops till they died; kept his policy and his peace till he died himself.

Henry VII. is noteworthy mainly for being but little noticed. The scribe of whatever time sees around him only that which is conspicuous and exceptional and often for the most part foolish, and therefore the documents of this Henry's reign are but few in number. The occupants of high places who are careful and prudent are rarely popular. His unpopularity was moreover helped on in various ways. Dynastic policy thrust upon him a wife of the busy unimpassioned temperament—a woman in whom deficient emotion and sympathy

and affection were not compensated by any high
qualities; a woman who was restless, mischievous, vain,
intriguing, and fond of influence. Elizabeth of York
had all the bad qualities of her father and her son and
had very few of their good ones. A King Henry in
feminine disguise without his virtues was not likely to
love or be loved. Domestic sourness is probably a not
infrequent cause of taciturnity and mystery and seclusion
in the characters of both men and women. It was
well that Henry was neither angry nor morose. It
says much for him moreover that while he was the
object of ceaseless intrigue and hostility and rancour
he yet never gave way to cynicism or revenge or
cruelty.

With a tolerably happy marriage, an assenting and
a helpful nobility, and an unassailed throne, it is difficult
to put a limit to the good which Henry VII. might
have done and which it lay in him to do. As it was he
smoothed the way for enterprise and discovery, for the
printing press and the new learning. He was the first
of English monarchs who befriended education—using
the word in its modern sense. It is curious that the
acutest changes in our history—the death of a decrepit
mediævalism, the birth of the young giant modernism—
happened in our so-called sleepiest reign. Surely the
" quiet" father had a smaller share of popular applause
than he deserved, and as surely the "dashing" son a
much larger share. But in all periods, old and new,
popularity should give us pause: yesterday, for
example, inquisitors were knelt to, hailed with acclamation
and pelted with flowers, and heretics were spat
upon, hissed at, and burnt, but to-day's flowers are for
the heretics and the execrations are for the inquisitors.

Thus then in all characteristics—intellectual, moral
and bodily—Henry VIII. must be placed in the

unimpassioned class. It may be noted too in passing that all the portraits of Henry show us a feeble growth of hair on the face and signs of a convex back—convex vertically and convex transversely. We do not see the back it is true, but we see both the head and the shoulders carried forwards and the chin held down towards the chest—held indeed so far downward that the neck seems greatly shortened. It is interesting to observe the pose of the head and neck and shoulders in the portraits of noted personages. The forward head and shoulders, the downward chin (the products of a certain spinal configuration) are seen in undoubtedly different characters but characters which nevertheless have much in common : they are seen in all the portraits of Napoleon I. and, although not quite so markedly, in those of our own General Gordon. Napoleon and Gordon were unlike in many ways, and the gigantic self-importance and self-seeking of Napoleon were absent in the simpler and finer character. In other ways they were much alike. Both were brave active busy men; but both were fitful, petulant, censorius, difficult to please, and—which is very characteristic—both although changeable were nevertheless self-willed and self-confident. Both were devoid of the deeper passions.

THE WIVES QUESTION.

NOTE IV.

It is affirmed that no one save a monster of lust would marry six wives — a monster of lust being of course a man of over-mastering passion. It might be asked, in passing, seeing that six wives is the sign of a perfect "monster" if three wives make a semi-monster? Pompey had five wives, was he five-sixths of a monster. To be serious however in this wife question, it will probably never be possible to say with exactness how much in Henry's conduct was due to religious scruples; how much to the urgent importunity (state-born importunity) of advisers and subjects; how much to the then existing confusion of the marriage laws; how much to misfortune and coincidence; how much to folly and caprice; how much to colossal self-importance, and how much to "unbounded license."

History broadly hints that great delusions, like great revolutions, may overcome—especially if the overcoming be not too sudden—both peoples and persons without their special wonder. In such delusions and such revolutions the actors and the victims are alike often unconscious actors and unconscious victims. Neither Henry nor his people dreamt that the great marriage question of the sixteenth century would excite the ridicule of all succeeding centuries. Luther did not imagine that his efforts would help to divide religious Europe into two permanently hostile camps. Robespierre did not suspect that his name would live as an enduring synonym for blood. But to marry six wives, solely on licentious grounds, is a proceeding so striking and so uncomplicated that no delusion could possibly come over the performer and certainly not over a watchful people. Yet something akin to delusion there certainly was; its causes however were several and complex, and lust was the least potent of them. The statement may seem strange, but there was little of desire in Henry's composition. A monster he possibly was of some sort of folly; but strange as it may seem he was a monster of folly precisely because he was the opposite of a monster of passion. Unhappily unbounded lust is now and then a feature of the impassioned temperament. It is never seen however in the less impassioned, and Henry was one of the less impassioned. The want of dignity is itself a striking feature in the character of passionless and active men, and want of dignity was the one conspicuous defect in Henry's conduct in his marriage affairs. Perhaps too, dignity—personal or national—is, like quietness and like kindliness, among the later growths of civilisation.

No incident or series of incidents illustrative of character in any of its phases, no matter how striking the incidents, or how strong the character or phase of character, have ever happened once only. If libertinism, for example, had ever shown itself in the selection and destruction of numerous wives, history would assuredly give information pertinent thereto : it gives none. Nothing happens once only. Even the French Revolution, so frequently regarded as a unique event, was only one of several examples of the inherent and peculiar cruelty of the French celt.* The massacre of

---

* From historic comparison we may feel sure that no such cruelty was found in the Gothic and Frankish and Norman blood of France.

Bartholomew was more revolting in its numbers and in its character. The massacre of the commune, French military massacres and various massacres in French history deprive the " great " Revolution of its exceptional character. But to return. There were licentious kings and princes before Henry, granting he was licentious, and there have been notably licentious kings and princes since: their methods are well known and they were wholly unlike his.

Certain incidents concerning Henry's marriages are of great physiological interest: a fat, bustling, restless, fitful, wilful man approaching mid-life — a man brim full of activity but deficient in feeling, waited twenty years before the idea of divorce was seriously entertained; and several more years of Papal shiftiness were endured, not without petulance enough, but seemingly without storm or whirlwind. When Jane Seymour died, three years of single life followed. It is true the three years were not without marriage projects, but they were entirely state projects, and were in no way voluptuous overtures. The marriage with Anne of Cleves was a purely state marriage, and remained, so historians tell us, a merely nominal and ceremonial marriage during the time the King and the German princess occupied the same bed—a circumstance not at all indicative of " monstrous " passion. The very unfaithfulness of Anne Boleyn and Catherine Howard is not without its significance, for the proceedings of our Divorce Court show that as a rule (a rule it is true not without exceptions) we do not find the wives of lustful men to be unfaithful. In the case of a Burns or a Byron or a King David it is not the wife who is led astray; it is the wives of the Henrys and the Arthurs, strikingly dissimilar as they were in so many respects, who are led into temptation.

No *sane* man is the embodiment of a single passion. Save in the wards of a lunatic asylum a simple monster of voluptuousness, or monster of anger, or monster of hate has no existence; and within those wards such monsters are undoubted examples of nerve ailment. It is true one (very rarely one only) passion may unduly predominate—one or more may be fostered and others may be dwarfed; but as a very general rule the deeper passions run together. One passion, if unequivocally present, denotes the existence of other passions, palpable or latent—denotes the existence, in fact, of the impassioned temperament. Henry VIII., startling as the statement may seem, had no single, deep, unequivocal passion—no deep love, no profound pity, no overwhelming grief, no implacable hate, no furious anger. The noisy petulance of a busy, censorious, irritable man and the fretfulness of an invalid are frequently misunderstood. On no single occasion did Henry exhibit overmastering anger. Historians note with evident surprise that he received the conclusion of the most insulting farce in history—the Campeggio farce—with composure. When the Bishop of Rochester thrust himself, unbidden, into the Campeggio Court in order to denounce the king and the divorce, Henry's only answer was a long and learned essay on the degrees of incestuous marriage which the Pope might or might not permit. When his own chaplains scolded him, in coarse terms, in his own chapel, he listened, not always without peevishness, but always without anger. Turning to other emotions, no hint is given of Henry's grief at the loss of son after son in his earlier married years. If a husband of even ordinary affection *could* ever have felt grief, it would surely show itself when a young wife and a young mother died in giving birth to a long-wished-for son and heir. Not a syllable is said of Henry's grief at Jane Seymour's death; and three weeks after he was intriguing for a Continental, state, and purely diplomatic marriage. It is true that he paraded a sort of fussy affection for the young prince Edward—carried him indeed through the state apartments in his own royal arms; but the less impassioned temperament is often more openly demonstrative than the impassioned, especially when the public ear listens and the public eye watches. Those who caress in public attach as a rule but little meaning to caresses. If Henry's affections were small we have seen that his self-importance was colossal; and the very defections—terrible to some natures—of Anne Boleyn and of Catherine Howard wounded his importance much more deeply than they wounded his affections.

If we limit our attention for a moment to the question of deep feeling, we cannot but see how unlike Henry was to the impassioned men of history. Passionate king David, for example, would not have waited seven years while a commission decided upon his proposed relationship to Bathsheba; and the cold Henry could not have flung his soul into a fiery psalm. The impassioned Burns could not have said a last farewell to the mother of his helpless babe without moistening the dust with his tears, while Henry could never have understood why many strong men cannot read the second verse of "John Anderson my Jo" with an unbroken voice.

THE LESS CHARACTERISTIC FEATURES OF HENRY'S CHARACTER.

NOTE V.

It is well now, after considering the question of Henry's parentage and organisation, to look again and a little more closely, at certain significant features in his character—his caprice, his captiousness, his love of applause, his self-will, self-confidence, and self-importance. These elements of character frequently run together in equal or unequal degrees, and they are extremely characteristic of the more markedly passionless temperament. But before doing this it is well to look, in a brief note, at some features of Henry's character which are found in the less impassioned and the more impassioned temperaments alike. Both temperaments, for example, may be cruel or kindly; both may tend to conservatism or to innovation; pious persons or worldly may be found in both. But the cruelty or kindliness, the conservatism or innovation, the piety or worldliness differ in the different temperaments—they differ in their motives, in their methods, in their aims.

The cruelty of the unimpassioned man is, for the most part, a reckless disregard for the happiness or well-being or (in mediæval times especially) for the lives of those who stand in his way or thwart his plans or lessen his self-importance. Such cruelty is more wayward resentful and transitory than deliberative or implacable or persistent. The cruelty of the impassioned man is perhaps the darkest of human passions. It is the cruelty born of hate—cruelty contrived with deliberation and watched with glee. Happily it is a kind which lessens with the growth of civilisation. Often it attends on the strong convictions of strong natures obeying strong commands— commands which are always strongest when they are believed to have a supernatural origin; for belief in supernaturalism is the natural enemy of mercy; it demands obedience and forbids compassion. Cruelty was at its worst when supernatural beliefs were strongest; for happily natural reason has grown, and supernatural belief has dwindled. The unimpassioned and the impassioned temperaments may alike scale the highest or descend to the lowest levels of character, although probably the most hateful level of human degredation is reached by the more impassioned nature. It cannot be denied that, even for his time, Henry had a certain unmistakable dash of cruelty in his composition. A grandson of Edward IV., who closely resembled his grandfather, could not well be free from it. But the cruelty of Henry, like that of Edward, was cruelty of the passionless type. He swept aside—swept too often out of existence—those who defied his will or lessened his importance.

How much of Henry's cruelty was due to the resolve to put down opposition, how much was due to passing resentment and caprice, and how much, if any, to the delight of inflicting pain, not even Henry's compeers could easily have said. His cruelty in keeping the solitary Mary apart from her solitary mother was singularly persistent in so fickle a man; but even here weak fear and a weak policy were stronger than cruel feeling. It was Henry's way of meeting persistent obstinacy.

It is needlees to discuss the cruelty of the executions on religious grounds during Henry's reign; they were the order of the day and were sanctioned by the merciful and the unmerciful alike. But Henry's treatment of high personages was a much deeper stain—deeper than the stain of his matrimonial affairs. People and parliament earnestly prayed for a royal son and heir, but no serious or popular prayer was ever offered up for the heads of Fisher or More or Lady Salisbury. Henry's cruelty had always practical ends in view. Great officials who had failed, or who were done with, were officials in the way, and *their* heads might be left to the care of those who were at once their rivals and their enemies. The execution of Lady Salisbury will never fail to rouse indignation as long as history is history and men are men. Henry might have learned a noble lesson from his father. Henry VII. put his own intriguing mother-in-law into a religious house, and the proper destination of a female Yorkist intriguer—no matter how high or powerful—was a convent, not a scaffold. In the execution of Elizabeth Barton meanness was added to cruelty, for the wretched woman confessed her impostures and exposed the priests who contrived them for her. The cruelty which shocked Europe most, and has shocked it ever since, was the execution of Sir Thomas More. More's approval would have greatly consoled the King, but More's approval fell far short of the King's demands. The silence of great men does *not* give consent, and More was silent. More was, next to Erasmus, the loftiest intellect then living on this planet. Throughout Europe men were asking what More thought of "the King's matter." More's head was the only answer. But however indignant we may be, let us not be unjust; Henry, cruel as he was, was less cruel than any of his compeers—royal, imperial, or papal, or other. The cruelty of our Tudor ruler has always been put under a fierce light; the greater cruelty of distant rulers we are too prone to disregard. We are too prone also to forget that the one thing new under the sun in *our* time is greater kindliness—kindliness to life, to opinion, to pocket. If fate had put a crown on Luther's head, or Calvin's, or later, on Knox's, their methods would have been more stringent than Henry's. Henry and his Parliament, it is true, proposed an Act of Parliament "to abolish diversity of opinion in matters of religion." But Luther and Calvin and Knox, nay even More (Erasmus alone stood on a higher level), were each and all confident of their possession of the *one* truth and of their infallibility as interpreters thereof; each and all were ready, had the power been theirs, to abolish "diversity of religious opinion."

There are two kinds of religion, or at any rate two varieties of religious character—both are sincere—the religion of the active and passionless and that of the reflective and impassioned. One is a religion of inheritance, of training, of habit, of early and vivid perception; with certain surroundings it is inevitable; if shaken off it returns. George Eliot acutely remarks of one of her notably passionless characters, "His first opinions remained unchanged, as they always do with those in whom perception is stronger than thought and emotion." The other is a religion (two extremes are spoken of here, but every intermediate gradation exists) a religion of thought and emotion, of investigation and introspection. It is marked by deep love of an ideal or real good, and deep hate of what may also often be called an ideal or real evil. Henry's religion was of the first sort. It would be deeply interesting to know the sort of religion of the great names of Henry's time. We lack however the needful light on their organisation, parentage, and circumstance. But in all the provinces of life the men who have imprinted their names on history have been for the most part active, practical, and unimpassioned men. They, in their turn, have owed much to the impassioned, thinking, and often unpractical men whose names history has not troubled itself to preserve.

And now, in the light shed by organisation and inheritance, we may gain further information on the more characteristic features of Henry's character—his caprice, his captiousness, his uncertainty, and his peevishness, his resolve never to be hidden or unfelt or forgotten.

THE MORE CHARACTERISTIC FEATURES OF HENRY'S CHARACTER.

NOTE VI.

HENRY was always doing something or undoing something. Whether he was addressing Parliament, admonishing and instructing subordinates, or exhorting heretics; whether he was restoring order in Northern England, or (with much wisdom) introducing order into Wales, or (with much folly) disorder into Scotland; whether he was writing letters to Irish chieftains or Scottish councillors, or Northern pilgrims; whether he was defending the Faith or destroying religious houses; whether he was putting together six articles to the delight of Catholics, or dropping them in a few weeks to the exultation of Protestants; whether burning those who denied the miracle of the Real Presence, or hanging those who denied his headship of the Church; whether he was changing a Minister, a Bishop, or a wife, his hands were always full. And in Henry's case at least—probably in most cases—Satan found much mischief for busy hands to do.

The man who is never at rest is usually a fitful man. Constant change, whether of ministers or of views or of plans, is in itself fitfulness. But fitfulness is something more than activity: it implies an uncertainty of thought or conduct which forbids calculation or prediction, and therefore forbids confidence; it is an inborn proclivity. Happily vigorous reasoning power often accompanies it and keeps it in check. In poorly endowed intellects, whether in men or women, fitfulness and its almost constant associate petulance harass many circles and many hearths.

It is recorded that when the disgraced Wolsey took his departure from Court, the King sent after him a hurried messenger with a valuable ring and comforting words. The incident has excited much perplexity and comment among historians. What was its meaning? what its object? Probably the incident had no precise meaning; probably it was merely the involuntary deed of an irresistible constitutional tendency; possibly, too, there lurked in the motive which led to it some idea of future change and exigency. The active, practical, serviceable man sows many seeds and keeps on sowing them. Time and circumstance mainly decide which seeds shall grow and which shall not. Caprice is not unfrequently associated with high faculties. Sometimes it would seem to be due to the gift—not a common one—of seeing many sides of a question, and of seeing these so vividly that action is thereby enfeebled or frequently changed. Sometimes it is a conservative instinct which sees that a given step is too bold and must be retraced. It certainly is not selfishness: a long-pondered policy is often dashed to the ground in an instant, or a long-sought friendship is ended by a moment's insult. At root caprice is an inborn constitutional bias. Henry was the first powerful personage who declared that the Papal authority was Divine—declaring this, indeed, with so much fervour that the good Catholic More expostulated with him. But Henry was also the first high personage who threw Papal authority to the winds. It is on record that Henry would have taken Wolsey into favour again had Wolsey lived. Not Wolsey only but all Henry's Ministers would have been employed and dismissed time after time could they but have contrived to keep their heads on their shoulders. Henry might even have re-married his wives had they lived long enough. One circumstance only would have lessened their chances—attractive women were more numerous than experts in statecraft: for one Wolsey there were a thousand fair women.

Habitual fitfulness, it has already been noted, is not often found apart from habitual petulance, and both these qualities were conspicuous in Henry's character. There was something almost impish in the spirit which led him to don gorgeous attire—men had not then got out of barbaric finery, and women are still in its bondage—on the day of Anne Boleyn's bloodshed. Nay more, there was undoubtedly a dash of cruelty in it, as there was in the acerbity which led him to exclaim that the Pope might send a Cardinal's hat to Fisher, but he would take care that Fisher had no head to put it on. Now and then his whims were simply puerile; it was so when he signalised some triumph over a Continental potentate by a dolls' battle on the Thames. Two galleys, one carrying the Romish and the other the English decorations, met each other. After due conflict, the royalists boarded the papal galley and threw figures of the pope and sundry cardinals into the water—king and court loudly applauding. But again, let us not forget that those days were more deeply stained than ours with puerility and cruelty and spite. More, it is true, rose above the puerility of his time; Erasmus rose above both its cruelty and its puerility; Henry rose above neither.

No charge is brought against Henry with more unanimity and vehemence than that of selfishness.

And the charge is not altogether a baseless one; but
the selfishness which stained Henry's character is not
the selfishness he is accused of. When Henry is said
to have been a monster of selfishness it is implied that
he was a monster of self-indulgence. He was not
that—he was the opposite of that. He was in reality
a monster of self-importance, and extreme personal
importance is incompatible with gross personal
indulgence. Self-indulgence is the failing of the
impassioned, especially when the mental gifts are
poor; while self-importance is the failing of the
passionless, especially when the mental gifts are rich.
Let there be given three factors, an unimpassioned
temperament, a vigorous intellect, and circumstance
favourable to public life—committee life, municipal,
platform, Parliamentary, or pulpit life — and self-
importance is rarely wanting. This price we must
sometimes pay for often quite invaluable service.

When Henry spoke—it is not infrequently so when
the passionless and highly gifted individual speaks—
the one unpardonable sin on the part of the listener
was not to be convinced. A sin of a little less mag-
nitude was to make a proposal to Henry. It implied
that he was unable to cope with the problems which
beset him and beset his time. He could not approve
of what he himself did not originate; at any rate he
put the alien proposal aside for the time—in a little
time he *might* approve of it and it might then seem
to be his own. The temperament which censured a
matter yesterday will often applaud it to-day and put
it in action to-morrow. The unimpassioned are prone
to imitation, but they first condemn what they afterwards imitate. When Cromwell made the grave
proposal touching the headship of the Church, Henry
hesitated—nay, was probably shocked—at first. Yet,

for Henry's purposes at least, it was Cromwell (and not Cranmer with his University scheme) who had "caught the right sow by the ear."

Henry had a boundless belief in the importance of the King; but this did not hinder, nay it helped him to believe in the importance of the people also—it helped him indeed to seek the more diligently their welfare, seeing that the more prosperous a people is, the more important is its King. True he always put himself first and the people second. How few leaders of men or movements do otherwise. Possibly William III. would have stepped down from his throne if it had been shown that another in his place could better curb the ambition of France abroad, or better secure the mutual toleration of religious parties at home. Possibly, nay probably, George Washington would have retired could he have seen that the attainment of American independence was more assured in other hands. Lloyd Garrison would have gladly retired into private life if another more quickly than he could have given freedom to the slave. John Bright would have willingly held his tongue if thereby another tongue could have spoken more powerfully for the good of his fellow-men. Such men can be counted on the fingers and Henry is not one of them. Henry would have denied (as would all his compeers in temperament) that he put himself first. He would have said; "I desire the people's good first and above all things;" but he would have significantly added; "Their good is safest in my hands."

It is a moot point in history whether Henry was led by his high officials or was followed by them. Did he, for example, direct Wolsey or did Wolsey (as is the common view) in reality lead his King while appearing to follow him. To me the balance of evidence, as well as the natural proclivities of Henry's character, favour the view that he thought and willed and acted for himself. Do we not indeed know too well the fate of those whose thought and will ran counter to his? No man's opinion and conduct are independent of his surroundings and his time; for every man, especially every monarch, must see much through other eyes and hear much through other ears. But if other eyes and other ears are numerous enough they will also be conflicting enough, and will strengthen rather than diminish the self-confidence and self-importance of the self-confident and self-important ruler.

Self-importance, as a rule, is built on a foundation of solid self-confidence, and Henry's confidence in himself was broad enough and deep enough to sustain any conceivable edifice. The Romish church was then, and had been for a thousand years, the strongest influence in Europe. It touched every event in men's bodily lives and decided also the fate of their immortal souls. Henry nevertheless had no misgiving as to his fitness to be the spiritual head of the Church in this country, or the spiritual head of the great globe itself, if the great globe had had one Church only.

When I come to speak of the Reformation I shall have to remark that, had the great European religious movement reached our island in any other reign than Henry's, religion would not have been exactly what it now is. Of all our rulers Henry was the only one who was at the same time willing enough, educated enough (he had been trained to be an Archbishop), able enough, and pious enough to be at any rate the *first* head of a great Church.

Henry was so sagacious that he never forgot the superiority of sagacity over force. He delighted in reasoning, teaching, exhorting; and he believed that while any ruler could command, few could argue and very few could convince. It is true, alas, that when individuals or bodies were not convinced if he spoke, he became unreasonably petulant. When Scotland did not accept a long string of unwise proposals he laid Leith in ashes. When Ireland did not yield to his wishes, he knocked a castle to atoms with cannon, and thereby so astonished Ireland, be it noted, that it remained peaceful and prosperous during the remainder of his reign.

Perhaps the happiest moments in Henry's life were those when he presided over courts of theological inquiry. To confute heresy was his chief delight; and his vanity was indulged to its utmost when the heretical Lambert was tried. Clothed in white silk, seated on a throne, surrounded by peers and bishops and learned doctors, he directed the momentous matters of this world and the next; he elucidated, expounded, and laid down the laws of both heaven and earth. It was a high day; one thing only marred its splendour—he, the first living defender of orthodoxy, had spoken and heterodoxy remained unconvinced. Heterodoxy must clearly be left to its just punishment, for bishops, peers, and learned doctors were astonished at the display of so much eloquence, learning, and piety.

The physiological student of human nature who is much interested in the question of martyrdom finds, indeed, that the martyr-burner and the martyr (of whatever temperament) have much in common. Both believe themselves to possess assured and indisputable truth; both are infallible; both self-confident; both are prepared, in the interests of truth, to throw their neighbours into the fire if circumstance is favourable; both are willing to be themselves thrown into the fire if circumstance is adverse. One day they burn, the next day they are burnt.

The feature in Henry's character which as we have seen amounted to mania was his love of popularity; it was a mania which saved him from many evils. Even unbridled self-will does little harm if it be an unbridled self-will to stand well with a progressive people. It has been a matter of surprise to those who contend that Henry, seeing that he possessed—it is said usurped—a lion's power, did not use it with lion-like licence. His ingrained love of applause is the physiological explanation. Let it be noted, too, that not everyone who thirsts for popularity succeeds in obtaining it, for success demands several factors: behind popular applause there must be action, behind action must be self-confidence, behind self-confidence must be large capability. Henry had all these. In such a chain love of applause is the link least likely to be missing. For, indeed, what is the use of being active, capable, confident and important in a closet? The crow sings as sweetly as the nightingale if no one is listening, and importance is no better than insignificance if there is no one "there to see."

We shall gain further and not uninteresting knowledge of Henry's character if we look at certain side lights which history throws upon it. We turn therefore, in another note, to look for a few moments at the men, the movements, the drift, the institutions of his time, and observe how he bore himself towards them.

HENRY AND HIS COMPEERS.

NOTE VII.

IN Henry's time, and in every time, the art of judging women has been a very imperfect one. It is an imperfect art still and, as long as it takes for granted that women are radically unlike men, so long it will remain imperfect. But Henry was a good judge of one sex at any rate, for he was helped by the most capable men then living, and in reality he tolerated no stupidity—except in his wives. In an era of theological change it was perhaps an unfortunate circumstance that he was better helped in his politics than in his theology. Wolsey, although a Cardinal and even a candidate for the Papal chair, was to all intents and purposes a practical statesman. Had he succeeded in becoming a Pope he would nevertheless have remained a mere politician. Wolsey, then, and Cromwell and More were all distinctly abler men than Cranmer or Latimer or Gardiner.

But Henry himself, looking at him in all that he was and in all that he did, was not unworthy of his helpers. There were then living in Europe some of the most enduring names in history. More, it is true, was made of finer clay than the king; Erasmus was not only the loftiest figure of his time—he is one of the loftiest of any time; but Henry was also a great personality and easily held his own in the front rank of European personalities. As a ruler no potentate of his time—royal, imperial or papal—could for a moment compare with him. Of all known Englishmen he was the fittest to be King of England. Had it been Henry's fortune to have had one or two or even three wives only, our school histories would have contained a chapter entitled "How 'Henry the Good' steered his country safely through its greatest storm." He played many parts with striking ability. He was probably as great a statesman as Wolsey or More or Cromwell. He would certainly have made a better archbishop than Cranmer; a better bishop than Latimer or Gardiner; he was a better soldier than Norfolk. What then might he have been had he been a statesman only, or a diplomatist or an ecclesiastic or a soldier only?

In all the parts he played, save the part of husband, his unimpassioned temperament stood him in good stead. A man's attitudes to his fellow-men and to the movements of his time are, on the whole, determined more by his intellect than by his feeling. The emotions indeed are very disturbing elements. They have, it is true, made or helped to make a few careers; but they have destroyed many more. Very curiously, Henry's compeers were, most of them, like himself—unimpassioned men. Latimer, who was perhaps an exception, preached sermons at Paul's Cross brimful of a passion which Henry admired but did not understand. Cranmer too was a man of undoubted feeling and strong affection. It is said there is sometimes a magnetic charm between the unlike in temperament; strong friendships certainly exist between them; and it is to Henry's credit that to the last he kept near to him a man so unlike himself. Cranmer was a kindly, sympathetic, helpful, good soul, but not a saint. He was not one of those to whom Gracian refers as becoming bad out of pure goodness. Cranmer was a capable and a strong man, but he was not supremely capable or supremely strong. He was free from the worst of human evils—'cocksureness.' The acute Spaniard just named says that "every blockhead is thoroughly persuaded that he is in the right;" Cranmer was less of a blockhead than most of his compeers. Left to his own instincts, he preferred to live and let others live. Cranmer had not the loftiness (nor the hardness and inflexibility) of a More; not the genius and grace and scholarship of an Erasmus; not the definite purpose and iron will of a Cromwell; not the fire of a Latimer; not the clear sight and grasp of a Gardiner; not the sagacity and varied gifts of a Henry; but for my part I would have chosen him before all his fellows (certainly his English fellows) to advise with and to confide in. Of all the tables and the roofs of that time I should have preferred to sit at his table and sleep under his roof. The great luminaries who guide in revolutions are rare, and the smaller lights of smaller circumstance are not rare; but—the question is not easy to answer—which could we best spare, if we were compelled to choose, the towering lighthouse of exceptional storm or the cheery lamp of daily life?

One figure of Henry's times which never fails to interest us is that of Sir Thomas More. More was clearly one of the unimpassioned class; but his commanding intellect, his quick response to high influences, his capability of forming noble friendships, and his lofty ideals seemed to dispense with the need of deep emotions. More and Henry, indeed, were much alike in many ways. Both were precocious in early life; both were quick, alert, practical; both were able; both, to the outside world at least, were genial, affable, attractive; both also, alas, were fitful, censorious, difficult to please; both were self-confident —one confident enough to kill, the other confident enough to be killed. Had they changed places in the greatest crisis of their lives Henry would have rejected More's headship of the Church and More would have sent Henry to the block.

In order to understand More's character correctly we must recognise the changing waves of circumstance through which he passed. There were in fact two Mores, the earlier and the later. The earlier More was an unembittered and independent thinker; the seeming spirit of independence however was, in a great degree, merely the spirit of contradiction. He was a friend of education and the new learning. He advocated reform in religion; but reform, be it noted, before the Reformation, reform gently and from within; reform when kings and scholars and popes themselves all asked for it. History, unhappily, tells of much reform on the lips which doggedly refused to translate itself into practice. The earlier More was all for reform in principle, but he invariably disapproved of it in detail. The later and in some degree embittered More was thrown by temperament, by the natural bias of increasing years and by the exigencies of combat, into the ecclesiastical and reactionary camp, and in that camp his conduct was stained by cruel inquisitorial methods.

The deteriorating effects of coflict (which happily grow less in each successive century) on individuals as well as on parties and peoples is seen in another notable though very different character of More's century. Savonarola, before his bitter fight with Florentine and Roman powers, was a large, clear-sighted, sane reformer; after the fight he became blind, fanatical, and insane. Why may we not combine all thankfulness for the early More and the early Savonarola, and all compassion for the later More and later Savonarola? Mary Stuart, Francis Bacon, Robert Burns, Napoleon Buonapart, and Lord Byron were notable personalities; they—some of them at least—did the world service which others did not and could not do. Yet how many of us are there who, if admitting to the full their greatness, do not belittle their follies? or, if freely admitting their follies, do not belittle their greatness?

Wolsey, holding aloof from religious strife, remained simply the scholar and the politician—a politician moreover *before* politics became in their turn also a matter of hostile camps. Being a politician only, he continued to be merciful while More drifted from politics and mercy into ecclesiasticism and cruelty. More's change was in itself evidence of a fitful and passionless temperament, of such evidence indeed there is no lack. His first public action was one of petulance and self-importance. He had been treated with continued and exceptional kindness by Cardinal Morton and Henry VII.; but when Morton, on behalf of his king, asked parliament for a subsidy, the newly-elected More, conscious of his powers, and thinking too, may we not say, much more of a people's applause than of a people's burdens, successfully urged its reduction to one half.

More was by nature censorious, and never heartily approved of anything. When Wolsey, on submitting a proposal to him with the usual result, told him—told him it would seem in the unvarnished language of the time—that he stood alone in his disapproval, and that he was a fool, More, with ready wit and affected humility, rejoined that he thanked God that he was the only fool on the King's Council. More, we may be quite sure, was not conscious of a spirit of contradiction. He probably felt that his first duty was to suggest to everybody some improvement in everything. This spirit of antagonism nevertheless played a leading part in his changeful life. In his early years he found orthodoxy rampant and defiant, consequently he inclined to heresy; at a later period heresy became rampant and defiant, and as inevitably he returned to the older faith and views. A modern scholar and piquant censor, and—I gather from his own writings, the only knowledge I have of him—an extreme specimen of the unimpassioned temperament, Mark Pattison, says that he never saw anything without suggesting how it might have been better; and that every time he entered a railway carriage he worked out a better time table than the one in use. If More had lived in his own Utopia he would have found fault with it, and drawn in imagination another and a better land. The later More was, as all unimpassioned and censorious temperaments are, a prophet of evil; and as much evil did happen—was sure to happen—his wisdom has come down to us somewhat greater in appearance than it was in reality.

The cruelty of the Tudor epoch has already been spoken of. Catholics and protestants, kings, popes, cardinals, ministers, Luthers, Calvins, Knoxes were all stained by it. Henry and More, we know, were no exceptions. But More's cruelty differed from Henry's in one important respect—there was nothing appertaining to self in it, except self-confidence. Henry's cruelty was in the interest of himself—his person, his family, and his throne; More's cruelty, although less limited perhaps, and more dangerous, was nevertheless in the interest of religion.

HENRY AND HIS PEOPLE AND PARLIAMENT.

NOTE VIII.

It is in his attitude to his people and his parliament that we see Henry at his best. His sagacity did not show itself in any deliberate or deeply reasoned policy, certainly not, we may allow with Dr. Stubbs, in any great act of "constructive genius;" it showed itself in seeing clearly the difficulties of the hour and the day, and in the hourly and daily success with which they were met. Henry and his father presided over the introduction of a new order of things, which new order, however, was a step only, not a cataclysm. They themselves scarcely knew the significance of the step or how worthily they presided over it. The world, indeed, knows little—history says little—of great and sudden acts of constructive genius. These gradually emerge from the growth of peoples; they do not spring from the brains of individuals royal or otherwise. If the vision of a ruler is clear and his aims good, he, more than others, may help on organic and beneficent growth. Full-blown schemes and policies, even if marked by genius, are rarely helpful and not infrequently they end in hindrance or even in explosion. The Stuarts had a large "scheme" touching church and king. It was a scheme of "all in all or not at all;" for them and their dynasty it ended in "not at all." French history is brimful of "great acts of constructive genius" and has none of the products of development. For Celtic history is indeed a sad succession of fits, and not a process of quiet growth. How a succession of fits will end, and how growth will end, it is not difficult to foretel.

The government of peoples is for the most part and in the long run that which they deserve, that which they are best fitted for, and not at all that which, it may be, they wish for and cry out for. A people ready—fairly and throughout all strata ready—for that which they demand will not long demand in vain. Our fathers, under the Tudor Henrys and the Tudor Elizabeth, had the rule which was best fitted for them, which they asked for, which they deserved—a significant morsel, by the bye, of racial circumstance. It by no means follows, let it be noted, that what people and king together approved of was the ideal or the wisest. It is with policies as with all things else, the fittest, not the best, continue to hold the field.

Henry and Elizabeth had not only clearness of sight, but flexibility of mind also, and would doubtless have ruled over Puritan England with success; it lay in them to rule well over our modern England also. Charles I., by organisation and proclivity, would have fared badly at the hands of a Tudor parliament, and, again as a result of organisation and proclivity, Henry VIII. and the Long Parliament would have been excellent friends. Hand to mouth government, if it is also capable, is probably the best government for a revolutionary time. Conflicting parties are often kept quiet by mere suspense —by mingled hopes and fears. It has been well said of Henry of Navarre that he kept France, the home of political whirlwinds, tranquil for a time because the Protestants believed him to be a Protestant and the Catholics believed he was about to become a Catholic.

The majority of historians and all the compilers of history tell us that Henry's parliaments were abject and servile. The statement is politically misleading and is also improbable on the grounds of organisation and race. It is one of many illustrations of the vice of purely literary judgments on men and movements; a vice which takes no account of physiology, of race, of organisation and proclivity. For we may be well assured that the grandsons of brave men and the grandfathers of brave men are never themselves cowards. One and the same people—especially a slow, steadfast, and growing people—does not put its neck under the foot of one king to-day and cut off the head of another king to-morrow. It is not difficult to see how the misconception arose: in a time of great trial the king and the people were agreed both in politics and in religion. The people held the king's views; they admired his sagacity; they trusted in his honour. If a brother is attached to his brother and does not quarrel with him, is he therefore poor-spirited? If by rare chance a servant sees, possibly on good grounds, a hero in his master, is he therefore a poltroon? If a parliament and a king see eye to eye, is it just to label the parliament throughout history as an abject parliament?

Henry's epoch, moreover, was not one of marked political excitement, and therefore the hasty observer jumps to the conclusion that it was not one of political independence. In each individual, in each community, in each people there is a sum-total of nerve force. In a given amount of brain substance—one brain or many—in a given amount of brain nutriment of brain vitality, there is a given quantity of nerve power. This totality of power will show itself it may be in one way strongly or in several ways less strongly; it cannot be increased, it cannot be lessened. On purely physiological grounds it may be affirmed that Bacon could not have thought and written all his own work and at the same time have also thought and written the life-work of Shakspere. Shakspere could not have added Bacon's investigations to his own 'intuitions.' In our own time Carlyle could not have written "The French Revolution" and "The Descent of Man;" he could not have gone through the two trainings, gained the two knowledges, and lived the two lives which led to the two works. So it is with universities: when scholarship is robust, theology limps; and during the Tractarian excitement, so a great scholar affirms, learning in Oxford sank to a lower level. So with peoples: in a literary age religious feeling is less earnest; in a time of political excitement both religion and literature suffer. Henry's era was one of abounding theological activity: Luthers, Calvins, and (later) Knoxes came to the front, and the front could not, never can, hold many dominant and also differing spirits. In Elizabeth's time Marlowes and Shakesperes and Spensers were master spirits, and master spirits are never numerous. No doubt as civilisation goes on great men and great movements learn to move, never equally perhaps but more easily, side by side: more leaders come to the front—but is the front as brilliant? Choice spirits are more numerous—but are the spirits quite as choice? Another and a less partial generation must decide.

"But," say the few observers and the crowd of compilers, "only a servile parliament would have given the king permission to issue proclamations having the authority of law." But the people, it cannot be too emphatically repeated, were neither creatures crawling in the mire nor red-tapists terrified at every innovation; they trusted the king, and he did not violate their trust. The proclamations, so it was stipulated, were not to tamper with existing laws;

they were to meet exigencies in an epoch of exigencies, and they met them with a wisdom and a promptness which parliament could not come near. It is physiological proclivities—not red tape, not parchment clauses, not Magna Chartas—which keep a people free. It is rather red tape, and not the occasional snapping of red tape which enfeebles liberty. If the non-conformists, who by the bye detested Romanism more than they loved religion, had not rejected the declaration of indulgence of Charles II.—a declaration which gave to Romanists leave of worship as well as to non-conformists—does any sane person believe that English freedom would have been less than it now is? In our time a body of men who hate England more than they love Ireland have, of set purpose, tumbled parliament into the dust: now, if a capable and firm authority were entrusted for twelve months with exceptional yet absolute control over parliamentary procedure, does any sane person suppose that the English passion for free parliaments would be lulled to sleep? Rule has often to be cruel in order to be kind. Alas, the multitude is made up not of Cromwells, is indeed afraid of Cromwells. In total ignorance of racial proclivities, it foolishly believes that a Cromwellian speaker for twelve months would mean a Cromwellian speaker for ever.

NOTE ON HENRY AND THE REFORMATION.

NOTE IX.

It is a singular misreading of history to say that Henry did much directly or indirectly to help on the Reformation of the Church in this country, although the part he played was not a small one. Neither was the Reformation itself, grave and critical as it was, so sudden and volcanic an upheaval as is generally believed.

Luther himself did not put forward a single new idea. No man is thinker and fighter at once; at any rate, no man thinks and fights at the same moment. Luther struck his blows for already accomplished thought. Curious ideas of unknown dates—for history reveals mergings only, not beginnings, not endings, and the student of men and movements might well exclaim " nothing begins and nothing ends,"—ideas of unknown dates and unknown birth-places had slowly come into existence. In Teutonic Europe at least, the older ideas were becoming trivial and inadequate. It was the northern Europe, which from the earliest times had been dogged in its courage both bodily and mental; the Europe strong in that reverence for truth which rests on courage, which is inseparable from courage, which never exists apart from courage; the Europe strong in its respect for women; strong in its fearlessness of death, of darkness, of storm, of the sea-lion, the land monster, the unearthly ghost, and which was strong therefore in its fearlessness of hell-fire and priestly threats. Celtic Europe, especially Celtic Ireland, slept

NOTE ON HENRY AND THE REFORMATION. 57

then and sleeps now the unbroken slumber of credulity. Credulity and fear are allied. Celtic Ireland was palsied then, and is palsied still, by the fear of what we may now call Father Furniss's hell. It is surely not difficult to recall and therefore not difficult to foretell the history of so widely differing races. Everywhere throughout Teutonic Europe, in castle and monastery, in mansion and cottage, the old-new ideas were talked over, drunk over, quarrelled over, shaken hands over, slept over. Everywhere the poets—the peoples' voices then, for the printed sheet, the coffee house, the club, were yet far off,—the poets, Lindsay, Barbour and others in Scotland; Langland, Skelton and others in England had, long before, pelted preachers and preaching with their bitterest gibes. Those poets little knew how narrowly they escaped with their lives; they escaped because they shouted their fierce diatribes just before not just after the strife of battle. They had flashed out the signals of undying warfare, but before the signals could be interpreted the signallers had died in their beds. Thought, inquiry, discussion, printing, poetry, the new learning, the older Lollardry had moved on with quiet steps. A less quiet step was at hand, but this also, if less quiet, was as natural and as inevitable as the stealthiest of preceding steps. Europe had gradually become covered with a network of universities, and students of every nationality were constantly passing from one to another. One common language, Latin, bound university to university and thinking men to thinking men. He who spoke to one spoke to all. The time was a sort of hot-house, and the growth of man was "forced." Reaction attends on action, but in the main, studious men made the universities — not universities the studious men; in like-manner good men have made religions, not religions so much good men. Ideas and opinions quickly became common property; sooner or later they filtered down from the Latin phrase to home-spun talk; filtered down also from the university to the town, village, and busy highway.

The Papacy itself had made Papal rule impossible to vigorous peoples. With curiously narrow ambition Popes have always preferred even limited temporal importance to unlimited spiritual sway. Two Popes, nay at one time three, had struggled not for the supremacy of religion but for merely personal pre-eminence. Popes had fought Popes, councils had fought councils, and each had called in the friendly infidel to fight the catholic enemy. The catholic sack of catholic Rome had been accompanied by greater lust and more copious bloodshed than the sack of Rome in olden time by northern Infidels. The teachings, claims, and crimes native to Rome, nay, even the imported refinements of the arts and letters and elegancies of Paganism did what legions of full-blown Luthers could not have done.

The Reformation, with its complex causes, its complex methods, its complex products, is, more than other great movements, brimful of matter for observation, thought, and inference.

The French Revolution was but one of a series of fierce uprisings of a race which rises and slaughters whenever it has a chance. French history teems with slaughters both in time of peace and time of war. Mediæval French Kings dared not arm their peasants with bows and arrows, for otherwise not a nobleman or a gentleman would have been left alive. At the close of the eighteenth century in France the oppression was heavy, the opportunity was large, and the uprising was ferocious. No other people have ever shown such a spectacle, and it is therefore idle to compare other great national movements with it. French history stands alone: no oppressor can oppress like the French oppressor; no retaliator can retaliate like the French retaliator. It is a question much less of politics than of organisation and race. But to return.

Mr. Carlyle, in his own rousing way and on a subject which deeply interests him—Luther and the Reformation—mingles fine literary vigour with an indifference to physiological teaching which is by no means habitual with him. The heaven-born hero tells us what has become false and unreal, and shows us— it is his special business—how we may *go back* to truth and reality. The humbler student believes that we are constantly journeying *towards* truth and reality—these lie not behind but in front of us. The school of prophets tells us that the hero alights in front of us and stands apart. The student declares that we all move together; that we partly make our heroes, and partly they make us; that we have grades of heroes; that they are not at all supernatural—we touch them, see them, know them, send them to the front, keep them and dismiss them at our will, or what seems our will. Carlyle affirms that modern civilisation took its rise from the great scene at Worms. The truths of organisation, of body, of brain, of race, of parentage would rather say that civilisation itself was not born of but in reality gave rise to Luther and the scene at Worms. The Reformation did not give private judgment; private judgment gave the Reformation.

In all revolutions there is a mixture of the essential and the accidental. During the long succession of the ordinary efforts of growing peoples there are also from time to time unusual efforts to bring to an end whatever of accident is most at variance with essential truth and reason and sanity and honour. In the reformations of a growing people, whatever the age in which they happen, whatever the religion or policy or conduct of the age, leading spirits rebel against what is most oppressive and resent what is most arrogant in that age; they reject what is most false and laugh out of court what is most ridiculous. In the sixteenth century men felt no special or inherent resentment to arrogance because it lifted its head in Rome; they looked on the so-called miracle of transubstantiation with no special or peculiar incredulity; their sense of humour was not necessarily tickled by the idea that a soul leaped out of purgatory when a coin clinked in Tetzel's box. Those were matters of accident and circumstance; they were simply the most intolerable or incredible or preposterous items of the century. Given other preceding accidents — another Deity, or one appearing in another century or arising in another people; another emperor than Constantine; other soldiers than Constantine's—and the sixteenth-century items of oppression and falsehood would have been there, it is true, but they would have been other than they were.

We are often told that great movements come quickly, and are the peculiar work of heroes. We are told, indeed, that from time to time mankind degenerates into a mass of dry fuel, and that at the fitting moment a hero descends, as a torch, and sets the mass on fire. Nay, moreover, if we doubt this teaching we are dead to poetic feeling and have lost our spiritual ideals. Happily, however, if phantasy dies, poetry still lives. Leaders and led, teachers and taught, are all changing and always changing; but no change brings a lessened poetic susceptibility or a lessened poetic impulse. If, in future, historians and critics come to see that the organisation and bodily proclivity and parentage of men have really much to do with men, let us nevertheless be comforted—the ether men breathe will be no less ample, the air no less divine. Every age is transitional—not this or that — and the ages are bound together by unbroken sequence. As with the movements so is it with the leaders: they are in touch with each other as well as in touch with their followers. All ages have some men who are bolder than others, or more reflective than others, or more courageous, or more active. At certain epochs in history there have been men who combined many high qualities, and who in several ways stood in front of their time. Wyclif was not separated from his fellows by any deep gulf, neither was he, as regards time, the first in his movement, but no leader ever sprang so far in front of the led. General leaders appear first, and afterwards, when the lines of cleavage are clearer, special leaders arise. Wyclif was a general leader, and therefore had many things to do. He did them all well. He was a scholar, a theologian, a writer, a preacher. It is his attitude to his age and to all ages, and to national growth, which interests us—not his particular writing, or his preaching, or his detailed views. He propounded, he defined, he lighted up, he animated, he fought. In one capacity or in two Wyclif might have soared to a loftier height and have shone a grander figure. But he did what was most needed to be done then and there. The time was not ripe, and it did not lie in Wyclif to make it ripe, for the Reformation, but he showed the way to the Reformation;

he introduced its introducers and led its leaders. The special leaders appeared in due time, and they also were the product of their time. An Erasmus shed more light than others on burning problems; a Calvin formulated more incisively than his fellows; a Luther fought more defiantly; and, a little later, a Knox roused the laggards with fiercer speech. It is interesting to note that the fighters and the speakers in all movements and at all times come most quickly to the front; it is for them that the multitude shouts its loudest huzzas and the historian writes his brightest pages. But let us not forget this one lesson from history and physiology: it is not given—or but rarely given—to any one man to do all these things, to innovate, to illuminate, to formulate, to fight, to rouse; it is certainly not given to any one man to do all with equal power, and certainly not all at once. For there is a sum-total of brain-force, not in the individual only, but in the community and in the epoch. In one stream it is powerful; if it be divided in several streams each stream is weaker. It was a theological torrent at the beginning of the sixteenth century, a literary torrent at the century's close. We have (perhaps it is for our good) several streams, we have however, we all hope, a good total to divide. Curiously, too, the most clear-sighted of leaders never see the end, never indeed see far into the future of their movement. The matters and forces which go to form a revolution are many and complex, reformers when striving to improve a world often end in forming a party. If the leaders are clear-sighted, the party will be continuous, large, long-lived; dim-sighted enthusiasts, even when for the moment successful, lead a discontinuous, short-lived, spasmodic crowd. Sometimes a leader steps forth clear and capable, but the

NOTE ON HENRY AND THE REFORMATION.

multitude continues to sleep. Wyclif, for example, called on his generation to follow him in a new and better path. He seemed to call in vain. In the sixteenth century men were awake, stirring, resolved; but no leaders were ready. Fortunately the people marched well although they had no captains to speak of. The age was heroic although it had no conspicuous heroes.

Although in its forms, its beliefs, its opinions, its policy, its conduct, there was much that was accidental, it was nevertheless inevitable and essential that the Reformation should come. It mattered not whether this thing had been done or that; whether this particular leader led or that; whether this or that concession had been made at Rome. If Erasmus could not fight Luther could. If Rome could concede nothing, much could be torn from her. There is, indeed, much fighting and tearing in history: complacent persons, loftily indifferent to organisation, and race, and long antecedent, are astonished that men should fight, or should fight with their bodies, or that, when fighting they should actually kill each other. In all times, alas, the fittest, not the wisest, has prevailed—and the fittest, alas, has been cruel. In the seventeenth century Parliament and Charles Stuart fought each other by roughest bodily methods, and Parliament, proving victorious, killed Charles. Had Charles conquered, and could Parliament have been reduced to one neck or a dozen, we may be quite sure that the one neck or the dozen would have been severed on the block.

When the thousand fermenting elements came together in the sixteenth century cauldron, no number of men, certainly no one man, certainly not Henry, could do much to hinder or to help on the seething process. This of course was not Henry's view. He believed himself to be—gave himself out to be—the fountain of truth. We know that he and an *admiring* (not an *abject*) Parliament proposed an Act to abolish diversity of opinion on religious matters. We know too, that while he graciously permitted his subjects to read the Word of God, he commanded them to adopt the opinions of the king. It was indeed cheap compulsion, for he and the vast mass of his subjects held similar opinions: Nevertheless, it is true that Henry, with characteristic sagacity, turned to the right spot and at the right moment when the cauldron threatened to boil over, or possibly to explode. At a critical epoch he helped to avert bloodshed; for in this island there was no war of peasants, or princes, or theologians.

Those who say that the great divorce question brought about or even accelerated the Reformation, are those who see or wish to see the bubbles only, and cannot, or will not see the stream—its depth and strength,—on which the bubbles float. For the six-wives matter was in reality a bubble, large it is true, prismatic, many-coloured, interesting, visible throughout Europe, minutely gossiped over on every hearth. If King Henry, however, had had no wife at all, the Reformation would have come no more slowly than it did; if he had had, like King Solomon, seven hundred wives, it would have come no more quickly. Henry was not himself a reformer, and but little likely to lead reformers. Under a fitful and petulant exterior the king was a cold, calculating, self-remembering man. The reformers were a self-forgetting, passionate, often a frenzied party, and as a rule, firebrands do not follow icebergs. If imperious circumstance loosened Henry's moorings to Rome, he had no more notion of drifting towards Augsburg or Geneva, than, a little later, his daughter Elizabeth had of drifting to Edinburgh and Knox. Henry had no deep attachment, but he clung to the old religion, chiefly perhaps because it was old, as much as he could cling to anything; he had no deep hatreds, but, as heartily as his nature permitted, he detested the new. He would have disliked it all the more, had that been possible, could he have looked with interpretative glance backward to the seed-time of Wyclif's era, or forward to the ripe harvest of the seventeenth century. Could it have been made plain to Henry that he was helping to put a sword into a Puritan's hand and bring a King's head to the block, he would have had himself whipped at the tomb of Catharine of Aragon, and would have thrown his crown at the Pope's feet.

He assumed the headship of the English Church, it is true; but even good Catholics throughout Europe did not then so completely as now accept the supremacy of the Bishop of Rome, and central ideas had not then so completely swallowed up the territorial. If Henry had not taken the headship of the English Church when he did, the Church would probably have had no head at all, and religious teaching in this country would have fared much as it fared in Switzerland and Scotland and North Germany. As it was, Henry simply believed himself to be another Pope, and London to be another Rome. He, the English Pope, and the Pope at Rome would, for the most part, work together like brothers—work for the diffusion of the *one* truth (which all sorts and conditions of Popes believe they possess), and work therefore for the good of all people.

Had the great European religious movement reached our island in any other reign than Henry's it would not have run quite the same course it did. Of all the Kings who have ruled over us Henry VIII. was the only King who was at the same time willing enough, able enough, educated enough (he had been trained to be an Archbishop), and pious enough to be, at any rate, the first head of a great Church.

But it is said: "Look at the destruction of the religious houses; surely that was the work of heresy and greed." Henry had no heresy in his nature, but he was not without greed, and as he was certainly extravagant, he had therefore the stronger incentives to exaction. But in our history the foible of a King avails but little when it clashes with the conscience, the ideal, the will of a people. Henry's greed, moreover, whatever its strength, was less strong than his conservatism, less strong than his piety. Stronger, too, than all these combined was his boundless love of popularity—a love which alone would have preserved the monasteries could the monasteries have been preserved by any single man. But new ideas and new religious ideals had come in, and the new religious ideals and the old religious houses could not flourish together. The existence of those houses had long been threatened. One hundred years before, Parliament had more than once seriously discussed the appropriation of ecclesiastical funds to military purposes. Cardinal Morton, after impartial inquiry, contemplated sweeping changes. Wolsey, a good Catholic, had suppressed numerous houses. It is interesting to know that at one period of his life Sir Thomas More thought of retiring into a religious house, but after carefully studying monastic life he gave up the project. It is not necessary to sift and resift the evidence touching the morality of the monasteries. Probably those institutions were not so black as their enemies, new or old, have painted them, nor so white as they appear in the eyes of their modern friends. But whether they were fragments of Hades thrust up from below, or fragments of the celestial regions let down from above, or whatever else they were, their end was come. Many causes were at work. They were coming into collision with the rapidly growing modern social life—a life more complex than at any time before, more complex in its roots, its growths, its products, and its needs. The newer social life had developed a passionate love of knowledge; it had formed a loftier ideal of domestic life. It pondered too over our economic problems, and disliked the ceaseless accumulation of land and wealth in ecclesiastical hands. Does any one imagine that a close network of institutions, which were at any rate not models of virtue; institutions which hated knowledge and thrust it out of doors; which directly or indirectly cast a slur on the growing domestic ideal; which told the awakening descendants of Scandinavian and Norseman and Saxon, that their women were unclean—that their mothers and daughters were "snares;" does anyone imagine that such a network could be permitted to entangle and strangle modern life? It has already been said that the newer social ideas were destined to arise, and that therefore the older religious houses were doomed to fall. It mattered little the particular year in which they fell; it mattered little who seemed to deal the final blow. Many centuries before, human nature being what it was, and social conditions what they were, quiet retreats had met a want—they were fittest to live and they lived. But a succession of centuries brought change—a little in human nature, much in social conditions, very much in thought and opinion, and the retreats, the inner life and opinions of which had not kept pace with life outside, were no longer needed, no longer fittest, and they fell. Henry did not destroy them. Catholicism, which neither made them pure nor made them impure, was unable to preserve them. Could the long buried bones of their founders have come to life again and have put on the newer flesh, thought, with newer brain, the newer thought, they would have found quite other outlets for their energy, leisure and wealth. It is so with all founders and all institutions. It is so at this moment with the institutions which were born of the Reformation itself. Naturalists tell us that the jelly-like mass, the amæba, embraces everything, both the useful and the useless, that comes in its way, but that in time it relaxes its embrace on the useless. So the civilisation of a growing people is like a huge amæba, which slowly enfolds men and ideas, and incidents, and systems, and then sooner or later it disenfolds the unsuitable and the worn-out.

QUEEN ELIZABETH AND QUEEN MARY.

NOTE X.

FEW rulers, few persons indeed, have ever been so much alike as our two rulers Henry VIII. and his daughter Elizabeth. No man was ever so like Henry as was the woman Elizabeth; no woman ever resembled Elizabeth so closely as did the man Henry. Both father and daughter were extreme examples of the intellectual and unimpassioned temperament. High capacity, acute perception, clear insight, correct inference were present in both. Both, too, were capricious, fault-finding, querulous and vain. Both, moreover, had their preferences and their dislikes. Both, too, felt and showed resentment when their vanity was wounded. But in neither of them, it may be truly affirmed, was there any consuming passion — any fervent love, or invincible hatred, or fierce jealousy, or overwhelming anger.

Those who preach the doctrine of an essential difference between the sexes and who, with the injustice which so frequently accompanies the abounding self-importance of masculinity, would deprive women not only of "equality of sphere" but "equality of opportunity," may study the character of Henry and Elizabeth with great advantage. Human beings are first of all divided (I have elsewhere contended) into certain types of character and only afterwards into men and women. Many men are by nature devoted lovers and parents and friends; many women

are not. Elizabeth was one of a number—a large
number—of women who have, it may be, many of the
qualities which tell in practical and public life, and but
little of the emotion which wells up in true wifehood
and motherhood and friendship.

Henry and Elizabeth stand far above the average
level of rulers. In sagacity, in tact and in statesmanship
only two of their successors can compare with them.
But the methods of Oliver Cromwell and William III.
were very different from the Tudor methods. Cromwell and William strove to be guided by what they
sincerely held to be lofty principles. Henry and
Elizabeth were guided merely, though wisely guided,
by the fineness of their instincts. Fine instincts were
perhaps better fitted for the earlier time, and lofty
principles for the later. It is easier, alas, to bungle
in formulating and in applying principles than in
trusting to adroitness and intuitions.

All the elements of character which Henry possessed were found also in Elizabeth, and many of these
elements, though not all, they possessed in equal degree.
They were alike in capacity, courage, sincerity, versatility, industry; alike in their conservative proclivities
and also in their love of pageantry—for Elizabeth,
like Henry, revelled in public business and in public
pleasures; she delighted in progresses, shows, masks
and plays. They were alike, too, in their sense of
duty, in their desire for the welfare of the people, and
also in their thirst for the people's good opinion. But
Elizabeth, although she had immense self-importance
(she heartily approved of the queen and, heartily
indeed, of nothing else), was perhaps less self-confident
than her father. She was not quite comfortable in her
headship of the Church—but then she had not been
educated for the Church as her father had been,

and she did not possess her father's devotional nature. Her conduct was however more decorous than her father's, notwithstanding that she was distinctly less religious than he—less religious in principle, in inward conviction and in outward worship. If she was less devout than Henry she had however a larger share of fitfulness than even he. The historian who more vividly than any other has placed the Tudor time before us speaks of Elizabeth's "ingrained insincerity;" the words "ingrained fitfulness" would perhaps be more correct, for she was in truth as sincere as her fitfulness permitted her to be. Although it is true she was not without—no one at that time was quite without—insincerity and intrigue and duplicity and falsehood in her diplomatic methods, she was fairly sincere in her views and aims and conduct. But unfortunately her views and aims and conduct were constantly changing. She was sincere too easily and too frequently. She had a dozen fits of sincerity in a dozen hours. Whenever she sent a message, no matter how carefully the message had been considered, a second was sent to recall or change it, and very shortly a third messenger would be despatched in pursuit of the second. Urgent and critical circumstance alone, and frequently not even this, forced upon her any conclusive action. I am compelled to agree with those who believe that the most distressing incident of her life was the final decision touching Mary Stuart's death: it was distressing on several grounds—she was not naturally cruel, or, like her father, cruel to those only who stood in her path; she did not like to kill a queen; and, above all, she hated to do anything which (like marriage, to wit) could not be undone. Elizabeth was compelled by temperament to be always doing something, but by temperament also she was always reluctant to get anything done. In her two bushels of occupation there were not two grains of performance.

Her extreme fitfulness had at least one fortunate result—it saved many lives. Henry's frequent change of view and of policy was unquestionable, but the change was slow enough to give to the ever-watchful enemies of a fallen minister time enough to tear the fallen minister to pieces. But if a minister of Elizabeth's fell, his head was in little danger: if he fell from favour to-day, he was restored to-morrow. He might trip twenty times, and as many times his rivals would be on the alert; but twenty pardons would be granted all in good time.

Touching the question of marriage the queen was far wiser than her father. Neither father nor daughter had the needful qualities which go to make marriage happy, and both had certain other qualities which in many cases make it an intolerable burden. Henry, unlike Elizabeth, did not discover this, for his perceptive powers generally were less acute than hers. She probably knew that in her inmost heart (her brain was sufficiently acute to gain a glimpse of what was in her heart and what was not) she was a stranger to the deep and sustained affections without which marriage is so often a cruel deception. She had admirers and favourites it is true; and, after the fashion of the time, was unseemly enough in her fits of romping and her fits of pettishness. But there has not yet been anywhere, or at any time, under the sun a healthful temperament which has objected to admiration and entertainment, and probably there never will be.

Elizabeth's attitude to the religious condition of her people marks a decided movement, if not an onward movement: for we must never forget that a multitude of high-minded and capable souls believe that the several steps of the Reformation were downward steps. But what were the steps, and what especially was Elizabeth's step? The popes (and their times) had said, *in effect,* you need not read and you must not think or inquire; your duty is to obey and believe. Henry (and his time) said, you may think and you may read, especially if your reading enables you to understand the King, but you must believe what the King believes and worship as the King worships. Elizabeth (and her times), still more at the mercy of rising Teutonic waves, exclaimed, you may think and read and inquire and believe as you like—especially as you insist upon doing so—but you really must, all of you, go to church with me on Sunday mornings. Elizabeth's churchgoing act, by the bye, is still unrepealed. Long after, William III. (and his time, though William was before his time) said, you may think, read, believe, and publicly worship as you will, but you must believe something and you must worship somewhere. John Milton, before William in time and long before him in largeness of view, was the one colossal figure who fought bravely and single-handed for freedom in every domain of thought and speech and conduct.

The Tudor time, more than any other in our history, lends itself to the study of character; a study which, although difficult, is the less difficult in that whatever of change may take place, old elements of character do not altogether disappear and entirely new elements do not make their appearance. These elements lie everywhere around us. A great writer and an acute observer of men declares indeed that we all contain the elements of a Luther and a Borgia (his ideal of the best and worst elements), and that if a man cannot see these near at hand he will not find them though he travel from Dan to Beersheba. The Tudor and the Stuart periods alike present remarkable persons and remarkable incidents; but in the earlier period the men and women were more striking than the events, while events attract our attention more than individuals in the later. With the Tudors men and women seemed to lead, for men and women were proportionately the stronger; circumstance seemed to be the stronger in the Stuart times.

No century contains three royal figures so striking in themselves and so clearly revealed to us as are the figures of Henry and Elizabeth and Mary in the sixteenth. Their capability, their vitality and their attainments would have made them striking persons in any position of life. Each, indeed, possessed the three qualities which make a really interesting personality—and such personalities are but a small proportion of the neutral-tinted multitude who are good and kind and industrious—and nothing more. They, the three personalities, could all see facts for themselves; they could all see the relative value of facts (the rarest of the three qualities); and they could all draw sound inferences from the larger facts.

The three individuals presented however but two types of character. Henry and Elizabeth were examples of one type and Mary of another. The Tudor father and daughter were, as we have already seen, not examples merely but *extreme* examples of the unimpassioned, ever active, ever visible class. Mary was as extreme an example of the impassioned, meditative, persistent and tenacious class. It was a remarkable coincidence that pitted two such mental and bodily extremes against each other. All sane human beings have much more of that which is common to the character of the race than they have of that which is peculiar to the individual. There was not only this common basis of human nature in Elizabeth and Mary, there was something more: both were singularly capable, brilliant, witty and brave (Mary being the braver and her bravery being the more tried). The two queens had certain unusual advantages in common, for both were educated to the highest ideal of female education—very curiously a higher ideal then than at any other time before, or even since, until our own generation; both, too, had much experience of life—the larger and the less elevating share falling to Mary's lot. But here the resemblance ceases. What in Elizabeth Tudor were slight though shrill rivulets of love and hate and anger and scorn and jealousy, or of pity or gratitude, were mighty and rushing torrents in Mary Stuart. We have seen what Elizabeth was: in many ways Mary was the exact opposite, for she was not at all given to bustle or change or acrimony or captiousness or suspicion. She was not, it is true, without vanity; she had ample grounds for having it and she was deeply human, but (it was not so with Elizabeth) her pride was even greater than her vanity.

The elements which met together in Mary were all of a finer quality than those which were found in Elizabeth; but in Mary some troublous elements were added to the choicer ones. In her high land there were ominous volcanic peaks, while in the decorous plain of Elizabeth's character there was a monotonous blending of vegetation and sand. In some of our greatest characters (the truism is well-worn) there have been grave defects. Burns' life never comes to any generous mind save with the deepest regret as well as the keenest admiration. Bacon's was a great

mind with a great fault. Shakspere and Goethe—the
two foremost spirits which time has yet given to us—
are not held to have led altogether stainless lives.
Now the Queen of Scots was not by any means one
of the immortals, but she was nevertheless and in
truth a great woman. Yet in the splendid block out
of which the ever-pathetic figure of Mary was chiselled
there came to light an ineradicable flaw. The good
and evil of all these characters were mainly, though not
wholly (for circumstance must not be forgotten), due
to organisation and inheritance. A little difference
in their organisation, and they would have been other
individuals than they were, and would most likely have
remained unknown to us ; but having the parentage
they had, and being what they were, a little difference
in circumstance would probably have mattered little.
What there was in each of organisation, what of
circumstance, and what of volition, is a problem the
solution of which is still far off. In all of them
volition, whatever that may be, did its best; organisation, let us say, did its worst; circumstance looked
on, helping here and hindering there,—the compro-
mise is history.

As the six-wives business clings to Henry's name,
so does the Darnley matter, though curiously with
less odium, cling to that of Mary. Henry has had no
friends save those who lived in or near his time. In
our time an inquirer, here or there, strives perhaps
to gain for him something of impartial judgment.
Mary has never been without warm friends, and her
friends seem to grow in number and in warmth. The
controversy still rages touching Mary's part in the
tragic event which inflicted so deep a wound into her
life. But although the controversy goes on at even
fever heat, the public judgment remains cool and

is probably just. It is kept cool and just by the weight of a few colossal truths which the deftest manipulation of a cloud of smaller truths cannot hide. At critical moments the physiological historian, who looks steadily at a few large incidents in the light of human nature, discovers clues which escape the vision of the purely literary historian, who is for ever diving — and usefully diving — into the wells of parchment detail. In reality it matters little whether this diver or that has dived most deeply; matters little whether certain documents are spurious or genuine. Mary Stuart accepted—she certainly did not reject—the passion of a certain man; that man was a leader among a number of men who murdered her husband; after the murder Mary Stuart married that particular man, and thereby most assuredly held a candle to murder. This was Mary. Now if everything that has been said in her favour could be proved, she would be but little better than this; if everything that has been said against her could be proved, she would be but little worse.

The student of historic characters never forgets the time the country and the circumstance in which his characters lived. We are now looking at a time when not only noble and ignoble characters existed side by side, but when noble and less noble elements existed together in one and the same character. For indeed the good elements of a better time come in slowly, and the evil elements of a bad past die a lingering death. The active Scotland (there was, we know, a good quiet Scotland in the background), the active Scotland of Tudor times was given over to factions, fanatics, self-seekers and assassins. Life was taken and given with scant ceremony. The highest personages of that time contrived murder, or sanctioned it, or forgave it—the popes did, continental sovereigns did, Henry did, Elizabeth did. The murders thus contrived or sanctioned or condoned were, it is true, mainly on behalf of thrones or dominions or religions, while the murder which Mary assuredly forgave, if she did not sanction, was on behalf of her passions. The moral difference between murder for a crown and murder for a love we may not now discuss.

It was to this Scotland, the active and factious Scotland just described, that the young queen of nineteen years was brought—brought from a different atmosphere and with an unpropitious training. The more favoured Elizabeth meanwhile was ruling over a quieter, a more united people, and was helped at her council-table by high-minded and unselfish men. It is useless now perhaps to ask if we may be allowed to admire the gifts, to deplore the faults, and to pity the fate of the more unfortunate queen. We can indeed, individually, do what we please, but the queen's posterity with no uncertain voice has declared that we may. Emerson says that the great soul of the world is just, and the great soul has kept Mary within the territory of its favour. It would seem that the affection and devotion which were given to Mary were not based on any single great or on any group of great actions; they were based (it is to her credit) on daily acts of kindliness and patience and unruffled grace. The sum of Mary's qualities, whatever they were, endowed her with the rare gift of making the world her friend; and the world does not, as a rule, make lasting friendships on insufficient grounds. Mary indeed, with all her faults, deserved a better country than Scotland; and England, it may be added, deserved a more gracious queen than Elizabeth. But whatever she deserved or whatever she was fitted for,

Mary's fate was destined to be one of the saddest of recorded time. Inward force and outer circumstance are so commingled that mortal reason fails to disentangle them. To-day men *seem* to put a curb on circumstance, and to-morrow circumstance *seems* to run away with men. An ocean of complex and imperious circumstance surged around two queens, one it lifted up and kept afloat and carried into a secure haven, the other it tossed mercilessly to and fro and finally drew her underneath its waves.

A number of leading Scottish nobles gave out and probably believed that the wretched Darnley's life was incompatible with the general good. Bothwell was but one of this number. Yet how clear it has ever been to all eyes, save to those of the blindly passionate actors themselves, that the Scottish queen's fatal error, even if there were no grave error before, was in marrying any one of the misguided band. But misguidance was in the ascendant. Could she by some magic web have concealed the husbands from each other and have married them all, she would at any rate have fared no worse than she did. But, to be serious, if a queen marries one of half a dozen ambitious assassins, the other five will assuredly make her life intolerable and her rule impossible.

In no aspect of character did the two queens differ more than in their attitude to religion. Elizabeth's piety, like her father's, though less deep than his, was of a similar passionless, perceptive, unreflective order. Mary's religion, like Elizabeth's, like that of all individuals in all parts of the world, was no doubt at first the product of her early surroundings; but with the Scottish queen it was much more than this—it was a profoundly passionate conviction and a deeply revered ideal. A living writer, who is perhaps unrivalled in the historic art and who rarely errs in his historic judgments, is less happy than is his wont in his verdict on the catholic queen. He avers that she had no share "in the deeper and nobler emotions;" yet almost in the same breath he states that she had "a purpose fixed as the stars to trample down the Reformation." To have a purpose "fixed as the stars" to trample down *one* religion was, in that age of the world, surely to have a purpose "fixed as the stars" to strengthen and protect *another;* to yearn to put down the Reformation was surely to yearn to bring in catholicism—catholic teaching and catholic rites and catholic rule. We may not be catholics, but we are not entitled to say that from an impassioned catholic woman's point of view this was not a high ideal; it had been the ideal of the judicial mind, Sir Thomas More, as well as the ideal of the enthusiast, Ignatius Loyola; it had been for a thousand years the ideal of a multitude of noble natures both men and women. Elizabeth, opportunely enough, had no ideals of any kind; ideals indeed are often inconvenient in a ruler; but she had, despite her acrimonious speech, plenty of sincerely good wishes and good intentions for all the world. If the Queen of England had no ideals she had many devices, and one was to check the flow of all sorts of zeal, especially Protestant zeal. In the two lives religion told in different ways—the difference was in the two natures, be it noted, not in the two religions. Elizabeth, with a skin-deep religion only, was evenly and enduringly virtuous. Mary had ardent and deep convictions, but her career was not one of unbroken virtue. Elizabeth was certainly unfortunate in her religious attitudes. She did not like the Protestants for she was not a good Protestant; the Catholics did not like her for she was not a good Catholic. In religion, indeed as in all things, she was greatly influenced by her inborn spirit of "contrariness." If the Catholics had intrigued less persistently against her throne and her life, and if (the idea is sufficiently ludicrous) the Queen of Scotland had chanced to run in harness with the hated John Knox (hated of both queens), she would gladly have given the rein to her Catholic impulses.

The two queens differed as much in body as in mind. I have elsewhere sought to show not only that certain leading features of character tend to run together (in itself a distinct contribution to our knowledge), but also that these allied features are associated with a group of bodily peculiarities, a contribution, if it really is a contribution, of greatly additional interest. Elizabeth, large and pink-skinned like her father, was by no means without impressiveness and even stateliness. She carried her head a little forward and her chin a little downward, both these positions being due to a slightly curved upper spine. Her hair was scanty and her eyebrows were practically absent. All these bodily items, as well as her mental items, she inherited from her father. Mary had a wholly different figure and a different presence; her head was upright, her spine straight; in her back there was no convexity either vertically or transversely. Her eyebrows were abundant and her head of hair was long and massive. All these peculiarities, too, we may be quite sure, she derived from her parentage (not necessarily the nearest parents) on one side or the other. In my little work on body and parentage in character I urge—it is well to say here—that the bodily signs of certain classes of character (two more marked and one intervening) are now and then subject to the modifying influences of ailment and accident, and especially when these happen in early life. In Elizabeth and Mary, however, no such influences disturbed the development of two strongly-marked examples, both in body and in character, of two large classes of women and, with but little alteration, of two large classes of men also.

[FOR INDEX SEE FULL TABLE OF CONTENTS.]

www.ingramcontent.com/pod-product-compliance
Lightning Source LLC
Chambersburg PA
CBHW020303090426
42735CB00009B/1205